PBF

Positive Behavior Facilitation

Understanding and Intervening in the Behavior of Youth

Edna Olive

Research Press ○ 2612 North Mattis Avenue ○ Champaign, Illinois 61822 ○ (800) 519-2707
www.researchpress.com

5   4   3   2   1   07   08   09   10   11

Composition by Jeff Helgesen
Cover design by Linda Brown, Positive I.D. Graphic Design, Inc.
Printed by Bang Printing

ISBN-13: 978-0-87822-544-6
ISBN-10: 0-87822-544-7
Library of Congress Control Number 2007932084

To my mother, Alicia Norma Johnson Olive, a woman who dearly loved the English language, teaching, and most important, her own and other people's children

Contents

Figures and Tables

Acknowledgments

Thank you . . .

- To my father, John M. Olive, who taught me through words and by example that I can do anything I choose to do.
- To my sister, Lea, who has always believed in her little sister.
- To my husband, Fahim, who never let a day pass without asking, "Is the book done yet?"
- To my mentor, Nicholas J. Long, Ph.D., who first taught me what genuine care for and effective teaching of troubled children looked like and felt like.
- To my friends, especially Lisa, Val, Donna, Deb, Charmyn, Sonji, and Shel, who loved me, supported me, and pushed me through this process, each in her own unique way.
- To my professional colleagues, many of whom I am blessed enough to call friend and teacher, especially Diane, J.C., Mark, Pat, Brian, Scott, Nancy, Erika, Cecelia, Frank, Larry, Steve, Jennifer S., Martin, and Rita, who share in the passion for this work.
- To my many spiritual teachers, especially Dr. B., Ron, Iyanla, and Chet, who see me when I can't see myself and continually teach me how to love as God does.
- To my dozens of spiritual brothers and sisters, especially Candida, Sonia, Poz, LaTonia, Candas, Beve, Tony, Claudia, Yolanda H., Traci, Debi, and Floria; thank you for your countless hours of coaching, thank you for your kindness, and thank you for your support.

- To my Australian mom and dad, Gary and Nita, who always treat me like a daughter and who generously support me and the work of ROCKET, Inc.

- To the thousands of people who have sat in my workshops and presentations, especially those who asked, "When is your book coming out?"

- To my fellow educators who still believe in the glory of serving children and who remain dedicated to the task.

- To the school systems throughout the country that have integrated PBF into their work with youth, especially the District of Columbia Public Schools, Baltimore City Public Schools, and Champaign, Illinois, Public Schools.

- To my accountability coach, who showed up at a time when the Universe understood and provided just what I needed.

- And to the millions of young people who laugh, who cry, who love their friends, who go to school, who play on playgrounds, who dance, who ride bikes, who chew gum in school, who struggle with learning, who talk too loudly, and who deserve every good thing from us.

Foreword

There is a critical need for a new book on the psychology of understanding and improving youth behavior. Most of the current books on this topic are either too theoretical and academic or too simplistic and fragmented. These observations are not true of this book. Dr. Olive has a keen insight into the complexity of youth and adult behavior and has responded by proposing a new, integrated strategy called Positive Behavior Facilitation (PBF). This is not a recipe book for adults to find the techniques to get George to sit down and do as he's been told. PBF is based on sound psychological theories and concepts that encourage adults to move beyond the management of behavior and supporting positive behavior to the skills of facilitating positive changes in student behavior. PBF is not a "quick fix" program but a philosophy to live, a set of beliefs to advocate, and multiple skills to use.

Dr. Olive's motivation for proposing PBF is based on her experiences and knowledge of the challenges faced by adults today who attempt to intervene in the behavior of children and youth. She is aware of the daily frustrations adults experience as they embrace the task of addressing youth behavior. She has taught troubled urban children and has served as principal to several schools for disturbed and delinquent youth. Most recently, she has supported schools and organizations, both nationally and internationally, by offering many services, including teaching, certification courses and training, and program development. Everything she proposes in this book she has modeled successfully. She walks the talk. She understands that the composition of youth behavior has changed dramatically. Adults must be prepared to support an ever-increasing number of high-risk and troubled youth who are often psychologically and physically neglected, rejected, and abused.

Dr. Olive writes this book to encourage the adults who serve children and youth who defy instructions, overreact to minor frustrations, and have poor social skills and little motivation to learn. Most adults have not been taught the skills to connect with these children and are forced to rely on their limited authority of obedience. Without an effective strategy for helping these youth, they are programmed for academic and social failure, rejection, and psychological alienation. PBF is the missing link that provides adults with a philosophical frame of reference, paired with effective strategies for succeeding with these youth.

I congratulate Dr. Olive for writing this innovative, realistic, strength-based, and reader-friendly book. PBF is a win-win for both children and adults!

Nicholas J. Long, Ph.D.
Professor Emeritus, American University
President, Life Space Crisis Intervention Institute

Preface

I developed the philosophy of Positive Behavior Facilitation, or PBF, because I decided to stop having conversations about behavior management. I made this decision because I realized I was inadvertently reinforcing something I don't believe in. I don't believe that adults should be primarily concerned with managing and controlling the behavior of children and adolescents. Now I know that's a startling statement, particularly in the face of the behavior being demonstrated by today's youth. But when I examined what I've learned from 20 years of interacting with kids and what I've read in the literature, something became very clear to me. Experience and research told me that when adults understand the behaviors they see from children, and when they learn ways to teach children how to make different behavioral decisions for themselves, their interventions are much more effective. Evidence proves that this kind of understanding and learning leads to more effective interactions with children than trying to force them into doing what we'd like them to do. And isn't that what we want? Most of us who interact with youth truly want to be more effective with them, whether they are our own children or someone else's.

This line of reasoning started when my years as a school administrator were over and I began conducting workshops about behavior. Much of the early work I did was the result of calls I received asking me to teach professionals how to make children, particularly those with challenging behaviors, do whatever the adults preferred them to do. Visiting schools and programs around the country, I saw the faces of hundreds of frustrated adults and even more faces of what the adults called "acting-out youth."

As I became increasingly alarmed by the seriousness of the behavior I saw and the reaction of adults to that behavior, I wondered what we were missing. I constantly thought about how I could support the children I observed and the adults who attempted to attend to them. To my surprise, while I contemplated how best to serve the adults who sat in my workshops, hoping I had the magic cure for the ailment of acting-out children, control and management became the focus of my discussions. As these discussions became more frequent, I became more displeased with the outcome of my time with these concerned, yet bewildered, professionals.

After dozens, perhaps hundreds, of these sessions, it finally became clear to me that my task was much bigger than teaching adults "tricks" to control children and youth so they could demonstrate the behavior adults determined was appropriate for them to display. Once I realized the significance of solely teaching strategies that manage behavior, I stopped having conversations about behavior management. Then I began having discussions about supporting positive behavior and behavioral change in children and youth.

The result of teaching behavior management exclusively, I decided, was that I helped adults create a need in children and youth to be controlled and managed by something or someone other than themselves. Instead of teaching the use of control as a tool for addressing behavior, my goal became to teach adults how to support children in becoming self-monitoring, self-managing, and self-aware human beings. I realized that anything less continues to put our youth at great risk for leaving their schools and programs in search of other people, experiences, and institutions that will control and manage them. While I contemplated how misguided my teaching had been, my years as a teacher and school principal reminded me that for many of our youth, those people, experiences, and institutions include gangs, drugs, and prison terms.

It was at this point that I began talking with professionals in ways that considered the following question: "What can we do to comprehensively and effectively address youth behavior and move away from mostly managing behavior?" My workshop sessions explored the topic of behavior beyond control of children and moved toward teaching ways that we can encourage the demonstration of positive behavior. My discussions began to focus on intervening in the behaviors of children in more thoughtful and thorough ways. It was because of these conversations and my repeatedly asking the question "How do I teach adults to facilitate positive behavior instead of only managing behavior?" that PBF was born.

After the birth, I behaved like most new parents who, in their euphoria, believe that everyone will see how beautiful their baby is. I thought that everyone would lovingly embrace my newborn and stand by appreciatively while I revolutionized the way adults understood and intervened in behavior. Instead, I quickly learned that teaching ways to support positive behavior in children and youth would be no easy task. Many of the adults who attended my sessions still wanted to focus on what needed to be done to control "bad" children and their "bad" behavior.

Inevitably, I would be asked questions that expressed a great deal of skepticism about the philosophy and strategies I offer in PBF. The participants in my workshops would raise their hands with doubting faces and ask questions such as these: "How do you expect me to teach my subject if I have to spend all of my time worrying about helping children make better behavioral decisions?" or "Why should I have to talk to kids about their behavior; isn't that what the social workers and therapists are for?" or "The school system that I work in doesn't address these issues, so why should I?" While I scrambled to think on my feet and answer these challenging yet valid questions, I wondered why everyone in the audience couldn't see the magnificence of my baby as clearly as I could.

I resolved to continue teaching what I believed in and committed myself to answering any question that was hurled at me from disbelieving workshop participants. In the midst of my resolve, there were times when PBF received great reviews, such as "Everyone in this school district should take this course!" or "This is the best workshop I've taken in 30 years!" During these moments, my excitement practically had me running around the room with enthusiasm. I encouraged the professionals who promised to take their new knowledge back to their programs to press forward even in the face of doubt, opposition, and the struggle that always presents itself when the topic of change is discussed. But there were moments when my own cynicism, despair, and hopelessness—fueled by those I was teaching—threatened to have me gather my transparencies, pack my bags, and leave the room with my head hung low. Yet PBF would not go away.

So at this moment, I choose to continue offering the message that we, the adults who care for children and youth, must do it differently or face the reality of continuing to lose them by the millions. This book, supplemented by the training sessions I continue to conduct, is a part of that offering.

By now I have accepted that PBF is not for everyone and that everyone who sees my baby will not find her beautiful. In an effort to help you decide if PBF is for you, I offer these comments for your consideration: Positive Behavior Facilitation is for those who care for children in any way. It doesn't matter what the role is—parent, administrator, teacher, child care worker, medical professional, or any other. PBF is for adults who are aware that we must do this with more intentionality, focus, and commitment than we've ever done in the past, and by "this" I mean the education, treatment, rearing, and support of our children.

PBF is for educators who believe that a part of their charge is building relationships with children and youth. This means PBF is for adults who are willing to know who children are and what challenges they face. It is for those who realize that without this effort, many of our children will never be ready to learn the academic content we are so eager to pass on. PBF is for those adults who embrace the journey of self-exploration and self-awareness. It is for those who are prepared to be truthful about what they find on the journey and are prepared to manage that which needs managing.

Positive Behavior Facilitation is for anyone who believes in the sacredness of children and youth. It is for those who understand, intellectually and emotionally, that children are precious and will act accordingly. PBF is for adults who recognize that a young life deserves our best efforts, at all times and under all circumstances. It is for professionals who can see the possibilities rather than the limitations imposed upon us by systems, politics, and the world at large. PBF is for those of us who are ready to take responsibility for what we do, what we say, and the results we create around us, including what happens to the children and youth in our care.

As this preface comes to a close, I end by addressing one of the questions I'm asked most frequently by my colleagues who are providing direct services to children around the world. That question is "This is great stuff, but where am I supposed to find the time to implement another program?" In response to this question, yet another extremely valid inquiry, my answer is this: PBF is not a program; it is a philosophy.

PBF is a way of looking at behavior and understanding what is seen. It is a unique and specific lens—one that allows for the recognition of what behavior shares about the life of another human being and encourages appreciation for the significance of that behavior. While PBF does include specific strategies and techniques to address behavior—and it does have its own language (see Appendix A)—it is much more than that. PBF is a frame of reference that, when adopted, can provide a set of attitudes, beliefs, and values that make it possible for behavior to be clearly observed. It also provides helpful interventions in the behaviors we observe. In addition, PBF allows for this observation and intervention to take place simultaneously with the adult's ability to be self-controlled. There is no time requirement necessary for the implementation of PBF. You don't do PBF—you live it.

So if you are still reading and you have not flung this book out the nearest window, Positive Behavior Facilitation is for you! My goal is to inform and encourage your endeavors while you inform and encourage children and youth. Through the philosophy, strategies, and techniques discussed in this book, it is my intention to offer you practical and functional information through what I call the "tools of PBF." I present these tools as necessary to comprehensively understand and effectively intervene in behavior. PBF deems that temporary interruptions (management and control strategies) of behavior are not enough. We must first understand what we are seeing and then intervene, depending on what children most need from us at that particular moment.

It is also my goal to deliver the message that this is not a losing war we are fighting with our children; in fact, it is not a war at all. Our children are a direct reflection of what surrounds them, and it is now time for us to address what we have created, no matter how challenging the effort may be. Fighting has not worked, coercion has not worked, building more juvenile detention centers and prisons has not worked, and ignoring the problem has not worked. Perhaps an honest examination of what exists, our role in its existence, and a realistic plan for what must be done can work. It is my hope that PBF can be a small part of what can work for you and for the children who need the nurturance, guidance, and committed service of all of us. Since you have chosen to continue reading, you will soon learn that this conversation is very different from the prevailing conversations about children and their behavior. If you are willing to embrace what is presented in this small volume, perhaps we will meet one day and have a conversation together.

*One part of the task is to help adults change
their behavior. . . . The other part of the task is to
help the child change her own behavior.*

—Nicholas Hobbs (1994)

Behavior in the 21st Century and the Role of Positive Behavior Facilitation

Now that the task of addressing youth behavior is clear—and PBF agrees that the task is twofold, as Hobbs has described it—the question is "How do we accomplish the task?" Let's begin by acknowledging a very important truth: The behavior of children and youth is different from what it was more than a dozen or even half a dozen years ago. Several years ago, Charles (2007) suggested that children are a reflection of the society in which they live and that they behave in accordance with the nature of that society. Almost 10 years ago, Lantieri and Patti (1998) told us that "we as a society are faced with the results of our cumulative indifference" (p. 3).

Regardless of whether you agree or disagree with the explanations of why our children behave in the ways they do, perhaps we can agree on a relatively simple fact: The intensity and frequency of behavioral incidents demonstrated by children and youth have increased greatly over the last 10 years or so. Why is that the case? As stated earlier, many believe it's because of the changing world and the times in which our children live and grow. Others believe it's because of the Internet and the influences our youth are exposed to. Still others believe it's the media; the music; and the disintegration of families, communities, schools, and even the world itself. Whatever the reasons, being able to encourage positive behavior in youth is one of the greatest challenges we face.

To make matters even more challenging for those who are up to the task, the methods we used just a few years ago to reach our children often prove ineffective for the children we are serving today. When our best efforts no longer work, we may turn to punitive and coercive measures to control behavior (Brendtro, Brokenleg, & Van Bockern, 1990; Brendtro & Shahbazian, 2004; Glasser, 1998c; Nelsen, Lott, & Glenn, 2000; Trulson, Triplett, & Snell, 2001), although research conducted over the decades has proven that these measures are ineffective and, in some cases, damaging to our youth (Dreikurs, 1968; Dreikurs, Cassel, & Ferguson, 2004; Redl, 1972; Skinner, 1954, 1973; Szalavitz, 2006). Even in the face of such research, statistics show that in the United States, we live in a time when many of our local governments build more prisons than they do schools and universities (Ziedenberg & Schiraldi, 2002). So the question remains: "What do we need in order to facilitate positive behavior in today's youth?"

BEHAVIOR AND NEEDS

One of the things we need is an understanding of the nature of behavior. A question that we must ask is "What need is this particular behavior meeting for the individual displaying the behavior?" When we observe the behaviors of children in particular, it can be challenging to remember that children are attempting to meet needs that are very similar to the needs of adults. Most of us, adults and children alike, have the same needs. These include the basic needs for food and shelter, and more advanced needs, such as the need to be of service to others, the need to feel some level of control in our lives, and the need to have meaningful relationships with others.

The majority of our behaviors serve the purpose of helping us to meet our needs, even those behaviors that we claim we would like to get rid of! There is, however, a major difference between us and the children and youth we are serving. Many of our children have learned to get their needs met by engaging in behaviors that are disruptive both to themselves and to others. The good news is that everyone can learn new behaviors that assist them in getting their needs met. This generally happens when individuals realize that the behaviors they are demonstrating are not serving their best interests. However, many children and youth have not been taught this lesson. Therefore, it's up to us to teach them how to adopt new and more functional behavior patterns. We must be willing to teach them how best to meet their needs with behaviors that are self-supporting rather than self-defeating.

An attitude that often hinders our ability to address the behaviors of children and youth effectively is the tendency to look for the quick fix. Try this exercise: Think about a behavior that you would like to change or eliminate. Now remind yourself of how long you took or are currently taking to change or eradicate that behavior. In some cases, we may have to face the fact that it has taken us decades to change a behavior! The purpose of this exercise is to remind us of one of the most important truths about behavior: Changing and modifying behavior that we have learned and are comfortable with does not happen quickly. It will serve us to remember that, unlike much of the food we consume, there is nothing "microwavable" about changing behavior!

Two of the basic requirements for facilitating positive behavior and supporting behavioral change in children and youth are (a) adults' willingness to be patient and reassuring and (b) encouragement from adults that children can learn more functional ways to get their needs met. Without these requirements, it is likely that both adults and children will be in a constant state of frustration with themselves and one another.

Another critical aspect of understanding behavior is the need to separate children from their behavior. Our behavior is not equivalent to who we are—behavior is something that we do, not a complete picture of us as people. However, many children and youth are viewed solely as their behaviors. This perspective can make it particularly difficult to support youth who consistently demonstrate challenging behaviors. Most of us would not want to be judged strictly by what we do. Before others make a decision about us, we generally ask that many factors be considered, such as our character, our words, our beliefs, and our attitudes. All too often, children and youth are not given this same consideration. When adults equate children with their behavior, it becomes almost impossible to see them as more than what they do. PBF requires us to see beyond the behavior of a child and consider who the child is in his or her totality.

PBF BELIEF STATEMENTS

What more is required from us in order to support our children and youth in learning and demonstrating behaviors that are socially acceptable? How do we assist our children in developing into self-sufficient and functional adults in today's ever-changing society? How can we facilitate positive behavioral functioning in our children when the odds seem to be stacked against them? What do we do about behaviors that appear to be practically unmanageable yet seem to be the norm among youth? If we intend to effectively address the behavior of children and youth, a well-equipped "tool belt" is a necessity. This tool belt must include a variety of techniques and information that will encourage the learning and demonstration of positive behavior. PBF can be supportive in that effort.

Before we examine the tools of PBF, it is important to understand that there is a philosophical foundation that creates the context for PBF. The belief statements listed in Table 1 can support us, first, in understanding behavior before we attempt to intervene in it. Second, they help explain how children, adults, and behavior are viewed from the PBF frame of reference.

It is important to note that these statements are offered not as a means to force any particular set of beliefs on anyone who happens to read about PBF, but rather to describe how PBF views the task of facilitating personal positive behavior and supporting children in doing the same. These 10 belief statements are not

TABLE 1
PBF Belief Statements

Statement 1

To be successful as an educator of today's youth, one must be fully committed (i.e., called) to do so. For these purposes, educator is defined as anyone who is imparting knowledge to children and youth.

Statement 2

Children are society's greatest and most precious resource.

Statement 3

Every child deserves our best and greatest efforts at all times.

Statement 4

Effective education of children in the 21st century requires awareness, tools, and skills that differ from those previously needed.

Statement 5

Educating today's children and youth requires awareness, tools, and skills that are diverse and multifaceted.

Statement 6

Many children and youth are wounded and are in need of healing. These wounds, including those that are very deep, can be healed with the support of caring and skilled adults.

Statement 7

Facilitating positive behavior begins with the willingness and ability to do so in yourself.

Table 1 *(continued)*

Statement 8

Healing ourselves of our personal wounds is directly related to our ability (or inability) to support children in their healing.

Statement 9

Our responsibilities to the youth we serve include extrinsic behavior management and creation of opportunities for intrinsic behavioral change.

Statement 10

The support and education of children are some of the world's most important work.

---

absolutes; they are guideposts that can help us navigate our way toward promoting self-supportive behaviors in ourselves first and in children and youth.

THE ROLE OF PBF

So what is the specific role of PBF in the task of effectively addressing behavior that Hobbs (1994) presented to us? The task has been contemplated for decades by the recent and not-so-recent founders of education, behaviorism, discipline, psychology, and conflict resolution. Several of these founders—including Hobbs, Redl, Wattenberg, Charles, Glasser, Brendtro, Long, Kounin, Dreikurs, and Skinner—have shaped the work of PBF. Each of these scholar's works plays a continual and specific role in the movement to encourage our children's mental, emotional, behavioral, and spiritual health. Similarly, it is PBF's role to offer a comprehensive and clear understanding of what behavior is and then to present specific strategies and techniques for intervening in that behavior. PBF is not a cure-all for addressing the challenging behavior of every child; in fact, no such thing exists. No one technique or strategy can address every child or every behavior. PBF does, however, play its role in this task by first defining behavior and then examining some of the components necessary to both manage and, ultimately, change behavior.

1

The [adult] is aware that he has no magic;
no quick fix to solve problems. He must
communicate to the student clearly that
not only does he have no magic; but he needs
no magic.

—William Glasser (1998)

Tools of Positive Behavior Facilitation

Even though some adults may argue that magic is needed if we are to support youth in demonstrating positive behavior, magic is not available to us. However, there are tools available to us, if we are willing to learn what they are and then practice what we have learned with consistency and patience. The six tools available in PBF (see Figure 1) include information and techniques that can minimize demonstration of inappropriate behaviors and maximize opportunities for demonstration of positive, more functional behaviors. Through use of the tools of PBF, we can promote our personal development as well as the growth of the children and youth we serve.

A SUMMARY OF THE TOOLS OF PBF

Tool 1, Awareness and Management of Self, allows for the examination and understanding of personal motivations and how our individual frame of reference impacts our interactions with children and youth. This tool also assists us in remembering that (a) we can address only those behaviors of which we are aware and (b) managing the behavior of others is impossible if we do not possess the ability to manage ourselves. This tool provides the opportunity to examine personal patterns of behavior and the thoughts and feelings that support these patterns. This examination supports self-knowledge, self-exploration, and self-correction.

Tool 2, Knowledge of the Dynamics of Conflict, teaches recognition of what takes place when conflict arises. Awareness

FIGURE 1
Tools of Positive Behavior Facilitation

Tool 1

Awareness and Management of Self

Tool 6

Effective Communication

Tool 2

Knowledge of the Dynamics of Conflict

POSITIVE BEHAVIOR FACILITATION

Tool 5

Surface Behavior Management Techniques (SBMT's)

Tool 3

Understanding the Differences between Behavior Management and Behavior Change

Tool 4

Healing Environment

of the dynamics of conflict enables analysis of the interplay between a child's thoughts and feelings, behavior, and the environment's response or reaction to the child. This tool also presents a detailed paradigm, the Conflict Cycle, which helps us understand how children and youth in stress can create stressful feelings in adults. In addition, this model teaches us the following important truth: If adults are unaware of or unprepared for conflict, they are likely to mirror a child's acting-out behavior.

Tool 3, Understanding the Differences between Behavior Management and Behavior Change, makes a distinction between what is needed from an adult to manage a child's behavior and what is needed from an adult to facilitate change in a child's behavior. Use of this tool allows for clarity about one's intentions when interacting with children and supports awareness that very different skills are required of adults in each situation.

Tool 4, Healing Environment, provides an understanding of the specific criteria and practices necessary for creating an environment that supports the growth and well-being of children and youth. Because so many of our children find themselves in environments that are wounding them psychologically, cognitively, emotionally, and physically, the healing environment is an extremely important element of PBF. This tool provides a structure for establishing an environment that will nurture and support children as they develop and, in many cases, heal.

Tool 5, Surface Behavior Management Techniques, or SBMT's, are effective in managing the surface behavior of children, or behavior that is generally visible and obvious. These techniques can be used by adults to restore, maintain, and promote order in the environment and increase desirable behaviors in children and youth. A major benefit of this tool is that it provides a broad range of strategies for intervening in behaviors that may impede intellectual, social, and emotional development.

Tool 6, Effective Communication, offers a comprehensive view of the verbal and nonverbal skills necessary for adults to be supportive of children and youth, particularly in times of conflict or crisis. This tool points out that communication with children requires more than casual conversation. Truly effective communication requires adults to master the specific skills of attending, observing, decoding, listening, signaling, and responding. By examining and practicing these skills, adults will learn the strategies necessary for effective and helpful communication. Tool 6 also describes the Listen, Respond, and Teach (LRT) method, which offers suggestions for effective communication between adults.

ASSESSMENT AND ACTION IN PBF

PBF is instrumental in helping adults to understand the differences between and necessity for assessment and action when intervening in the behavior of children and youth. Nelson, Roberts, Mathur, and Rutherford (1999) suggest that adults are often lacking when required to conduct effective assessments and develop effective interventions in response to children's behavior. As adults, we are often quick to act when we believe an action is required from us. There are times when our actions are based on necessity, and in some cases, our actions are based on our personal emotions. PBF asks us to conduct assessments that focus on what best meets the needs of children before we take action.

The tools of PBF that assist us in making knowledgeable assessments are tool numbers 1, 2, and 3: Awareness and Management of Self, Knowledge of the Dynamics of Conflict, and Understanding the Differences between Behavior Management and Behavior Change. These tools allow us to examine the details involved in challenging situations for ourselves and the children we are serving. In practicing with these tools, we take evaluations of ourselves, the children and youth involved, and the conditions of the behavioral occurrence—and we determine what subsequent steps are most appropriate for us to take.

Tool numbers 4, 5, and 6 are action tools. These are the Healing Environment, Surface Behavior Management Techniques

(SBMT's), and Effective Communication. Embedded in these three tools are processes, strategies, and techniques that support us in taking appropriate action in order to best meet the needs of children. By making the distinction between assessment and action tools (see Figure 2), we can use PBF more effectively and purposefully as we address the behavior we see from others.

Ayers (1995) tells us that the thoughtfulness required by those of us who have chosen to support children and youth requires "wide-awakeness"—a willingness to look at our lives, to consider possibilities and alternatives, and to connect our actions with our consciousness. The information and tools presented here compel us to consider our behavior thoughtfully and to be fully conscious in our interactions with children and youth. In the absence of what may be some much-hoped-for magic, with willingness, information, and tools, PBF allows us to act on our good intentions and make significant contributions in the lives of children.

FIGURE 2
Assessment and Action in Positive Behavior Facilitation

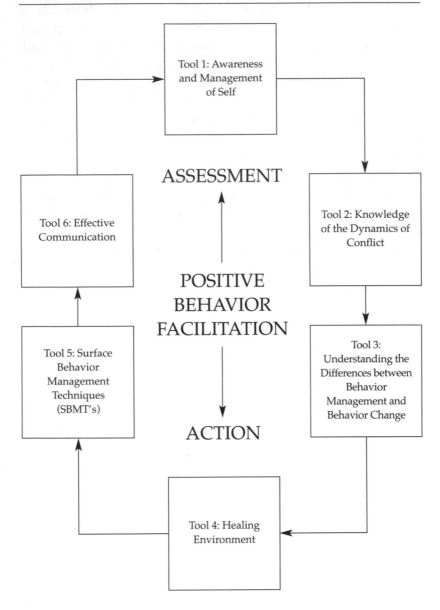

2

Teaching holds a mirror to the soul. If I am willing to look in that mirror and not run from what I see, I have a chance to gain self-knowledge—and knowing myself is as crucial to good teaching as knowing my students and my subject. The work required to "know thyself" is neither selfish nor narcissistic. Whatever self-knowledge we attain as teachers will serve our students and our scholarship well. Good teaching requires self-knowledge; it is a secret hidden in plain sight.

—Parker J. Palmer (1998)

Tool 1: Awareness and Management of Self

This chapter speaks to the importance of the first tool of PBF: Awareness and Management of Self. Facilitation of positive behavior in others requires us first to assess ourselves and examine our own behavior. It is challenging—if not impossible—to do for someone else what we cannot or will not do for ourselves. By becoming aware of and managing ourselves, we can learn the impact of our thoughts and feelings on our behaviors. This information can then assist us in encouraging children and youth to understand themselves. Awareness is the foundation of understanding ourselves and, ultimately, all behavioral change.

THE IMPORTANCE OF SELF-AWARENESS

Awareness is defined as a state of being informed, alert, and knowledgeable. Awareness is also often used to refer to a level of consciousness one has about something in particular. Goleman (1995) refers to this state of consciousness as self-awareness and defines this state as an ongoing attention to one's internal states. He further asserts that this state of awareness allows us to be self-reflective, even when our emotions are unsteady, and it enables us to move out of the emotional moods that are unpleasant or unproductive for us. As it relates to our awareness of ourselves, being conscious means that in this state of observation, we are attentive to ourselves and what we notice about ourselves.

When faced with the challenging behaviors that children and youth display, self-awareness can support us by helping us assess our current state of being and level of need; in other words, self-awareness allows us to realize a level of psychological insight (Goleman, 1995). Without this insight, it is extremely difficult for us to assess a child's state of being and level of need. Awareness must take place on the internal level before it can be effective on the external level.

A critical part of our service to children and youth is to provide for their needs and to be attentive to their state of being. Being self-aware will allow us to identify insights and information that are personally important to us. Once we become self-aware, we can identify insights and information that are important to the children we serve. When we are truly self-aware, we are prepared for our interactions with children.

While becoming aware of ourselves as individuals and recognizing our patterns is the first step in creating positive relationships with children and youth, managing what we have become aware of is the next step when we are addressing our own behavior. We must be willing and able to manage ourselves, particularly our behavior, when we are face-to-face with children. Managing ourselves indicates that we have some level of control and influence over what we present to others. When we learn to manage ourselves, we are able to regulate our own behavior regardless of the circumstances and what others may be doing or saying.

In his book *Choice Theory: A New Psychology of Personal Freedom*, Glasser (1998a) tells us that in order to understand our own behavior, we must broaden our definition and understanding of behavior. Glasser asserts that behavior has several components that must be examined if we are to understand its cause: activity, thinking, feeling, and physiology. He uses the term *total behavior* to refer to our observable acts of behavior.

Research also indicates that behavior is often a needs-based response or reaction to a specific experience or circumstance. In managing our behavior, we must also pay close attention to our attitudes and core beliefs if we are to assist the children in our care to do the same. It is much easier to be attentive to the events and circumstances happening outside of ourselves. However, in order to facilitate positive behavior in children, we must be willing to pay attention to how we function as individuals and how our internal landscape influences what we do. This recognition enables us to be aware of what we bring to the relationships we form with children.

THE IMPORTANCE OF SELF-MANAGEMENT

Self-management is particularly important in our relationships with children and youth when we realize the extent to which they have difficulty managing themselves. Many children are challenged when it comes to managing what they say, what they do, and how they interact with others, particularly adults. Therefore, another reason management of our feelings and behavior is so critical is that our children are watching us in hopes of learning how to manage themselves. Children are constantly watching us. Through observation, they learn how to speak, how to behave, and how to handle themselves, particularly in times of conflict. The question is not "Are we our children's teachers?" The fact is that we are always teaching something when we are in the presence of children. The more accurate question is "Are we teaching our children what we actually want them to learn?"

Managing ourselves also requires us to identify personal strategies for coping with our feelings. Children are often flooded with feelings, and while they may not be able to tell us how they are feeling, they can certainly show us how they are feeling. These demonstrations can create a variety of feelings in us, and we must be able to manage the personal feelings that arise. When feelings occur in children and in adults, a particular behavior will usually be demonstrated on the basis of our characteristic ways of thinking, feeling, and behaving. These characteristic ways are generated largely by our personalities and our individual personality types. Knowing ourselves and our general patterns of thinking, feeling, and behaving will assist us in making sure that we, and not our emotions, are in control of our behaviors. Self-awareness, when paired with the management of our feelings and thoughts, allows us to engage in interactions that are supportive of positive behaviors.

COMPONENTS OF THE LADDER OF SELF-KNOWLEDGE

The Ladder of Self-Knowledge (see Figure 3) is a visual synthesis of several factors that support our self-awareness. Knowing how we demonstrate these components can help us better understand who we are, why we behave in certain ways, and how our behavior affects others. When we are not aware and do not manage ourselves, we may demonstrate the very behaviors we do not want to see from children. Once we have demonstrated behaviors we do not want to see from children, we reinforce the likelihood that they are learning to behave in ways that run counter to what we are attempting to teach them.

In an effort to travel toward this necessary self-awareness, PBF examines several components that affect an individual's behavior. These include attitudes, core beliefs, mental and emotional triggers, thoughts and feelings, and defense mechanisms. However, before we go any further, let us consider a definition of behavior. Behavior is the manner in which one conducts oneself—the particular way in which one acts, functions, or reacts. Behavior is generally referred to as the acts that are observable. Often behavior is a needs-based response or reaction to a particular circumstance, occurrence, or experience. Using the analogy of an individual's being like an iceberg in the ocean, behavior is what is "above the waterline." As mentioned earlier, Glasser (1998a) has expanded the word *behavior* into the term *total behavior,* which includes acting, thinking, feeling, and the physiology associated with one's actions, thoughts, and feelings. Once we are able to understand the concept of behavior, we can begin to examine what contributes to someone's behavior.

An attitude is defined as a state of mind in relation to some matter or situation—a mental and/or emotional position toward

FIGURE 3
Ladder of Self-Knowledge

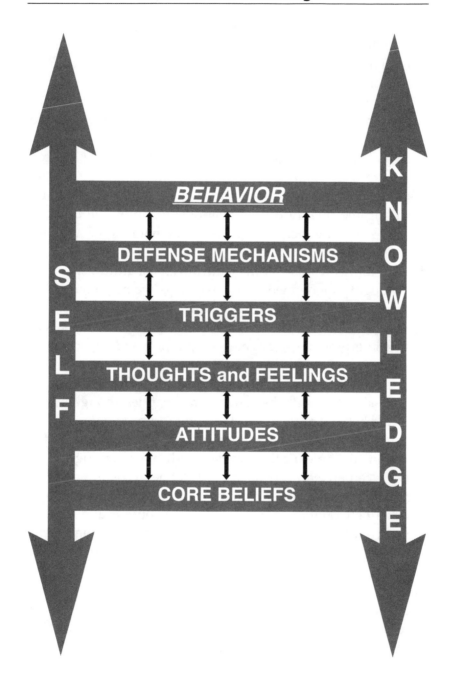

a fact or state of being. Our attitudes are supported by our beliefs. Attitudes can be changed and altered when we make new decisions about what kind of lives we would like to lead and what works or does not work for us and in our lives.

A belief is defined as an acceptance of an idea or concept as true—a precept that can function consciously or unconsciously. Beliefs are often associated with established family, cultural, racial, religious, and societal norms. We often accept beliefs as fact without questioning their validity because they are passed on to us by people and institutions we love and trust. Beliefs are often fueled by emotions and can directly influence our choices. There are usually three or four core beliefs that we hold as absolute truth and that govern much of the activity of our lives, including the quality of our relationships, how we think of ourselves and interact with others, and what kind of work we do. Beliefs are more challenging to change than attitudes, and three or four core beliefs can create dozens of attitudes.

Thoughts are defined as the meanings we make out of the sensory data we receive, primarily from other people and experiences. Thoughts are most often based on our needs, beliefs, values, interpretations, judgments, opinions, and expectations. Feelings are our spontaneous or programmed reactions to the sensory data we receive. Our feelings directly affect what actions we will take. Although they are separate entities, thoughts, feelings, and behaviors are in constant interaction.

Mental and emotional triggers are most often understood as something or someone that exists outside of us that triggers, or causes, a certain reaction from us. PBF defines triggers as internal and subjective responses to one or more perceived conflicts, based largely on thoughts and feelings. Thoughts and feelings serve as our filters and are developed in response to the memories, interpretations, and judgments we have attached to our life experiences (Vanzant, 2000). Each time we experience an event that triggers our thoughts or feelings in ways that we find uncomfortable or negative, or that cause us to be in resistance, we experience an emotional or mental upset. Our self-created unconscious and internal attachments to our life experiences activate the upset and serve as our triggers. This definition of triggers is different from most because it places the responsibility for what we think, how we feel, and what we do squarely on our own shoulders. Using this definition, we cannot make someone or something else external to us responsible for our behavior.

Defense mechanisms, listed in Table 2, also influence our behavior. When feelings arise in us that make us uncomfortable, we use defense mechanisms to protect us from the discomfort and to help us remain in a state of emotional equilibrium. The use of defense mechanisms is not dysfunctional. However, when defense mechanisms are the only methods we use to manage uncomfortable feelings, these coping strategies can prevent us from examining the true source of the discomfort and from learning to effectively handle situations that make us anxious. The knowledge of defense mechanisms becomes particularly important when we consider the behavior of children and youth who are often uncomfortable and anxious. When we begin to recognize the defenses that we use, we become more aware of the defenses children use to remain comfortable.

Defense mechanisms are also called mental mechanisms because they are born and nurtured in our minds. These are defensive behaviors that we use for compensation, protection, justification, and retreat. In all cases, we are defending against the inner self. The object is prevention of discomfort and inner conflict and the establishment of inner peace. Everyone uses defense mechanisms from time to time; the use of these defenses does not make us pathological or disturbed. As stated earlier, these mechanisms become a problem when their repeated use does not allow us to identify and examine the true sources of our stress.

In becoming self-aware, we must consider who we are, what contributes to our uniqueness, and how that individuality is presented to others through our observable behavior. Once we can become aware of how our values, beliefs, attitudes, thoughts, feelings, triggers, and defenses affect us, we can take the next step toward knowing who we are: self-management. Mastery of managing what you become aware of also allows for self-monitoring and self-correction, when necessary.

TABLE 2
Common Defense Mechanisms

Denial

Defending against painful feelings by not recognizing their sources.

Rationalization

A conscious effort to defend an action that has produced a feeling of guilt by coming up with "a good reason" for the behavior instead of facing the true reason for the behavior.

Projection

Another form of alibi—shifting blame to someone or something else; attributing one's own feelings to another (e.g., "I'm not mad at you—YOU hate me!").

Withdrawal

A form of escape—involves emotional, intellectual, and/or physical retreat from a situation perceived as uncomfortable or threatening.

Displacement

Transferring an emotional reaction to a substitute when it cannot be directed toward the original stimulus of the reaction.

Sublimation

Changing the direction of one's drive toward a worthy and acceptable goal (e.g., the school bully becomes the star football player). This mechanism lies behind many success stories.

Intellectualization

Another form of escape—the affective or emotional charge in a hurtful or threatening situation is cut off or minimized; feelings that are unacceptable or painful are separated and are tightly compartmentalized.

Conversion

Transferring distress to a physical manifestation, such as psychosomatic illness or pain.

Identification

When a person feels uncomfortable, threatened, or inadequate, overidentification with some eminent person or institution; the person may imitate the mannerisms or habits of others.

Regression

Retreating from one's responsibilities and problems by returning to the comfort of earlier years and engaging in behavior reminiscent of those times (e.g., rocking, thumb sucking).

STRATEGIES FOR SELF-MANAGEMENT

Self-management requires that we remember and practice our knowledge of the following points:

- There is a difference between reacting and responding. *Reacting* is based on emotion and feelings, while *responding* is based on logical thought. Feelings are the basis of reacting and often overreacting. Managing our feelings is part of our responsibility in managing ourselves. We can learn to respond to other people and situations in our lives instead of reacting or overreacting to them.

- All feelings are acceptable; it's what we do with them that must be managed. Everyone, including you, has a right to feel as they do!

- Feelings and thoughts interact with each other constantly. Our feelings influence our thoughts, and our thoughts influence our feelings. We can make choices to change or redirect our feelings and thoughts regardless of the outward circumstances.

- Events will take place that will evoke certain thoughts and feelings. Managing yourself means being prepared for these events. You can use self-talk as a way of accepting, expressing, and supporting yourself.

- It is important to be a thermostat and not a thermometer (Long, 2000). You can set the emotional and mental climate for yourself and not merely react to the "temperature" set by others.

- Acknowledge and accept your thoughts and feelings. Do not deny what you are thinking and feeling. Denial of your thoughts and feelings can cause mental and emotional upsets (i.e., triggers) to develop.

- When an event has not been resolved as you would have liked, resist turning any anger or guilt inward or outward, toward others. Instead, accept that things did not go well and that challenging events will take time and effort to resolve. It is important to be honest with yourself and others about what you are feeling and thinking.

- Allow yourself to take pride in your accomplishments when you have successfully supported yourself or someone else.

- Using *healthy* coping mechanisms is key to helping you self-manage, particularly in times of stress, conflict, or crisis.

DOMINANT PERSONALITY TYPES

Effective self-management can also be assisted by your awareness of your dominant personality type and the personality types of others. In recent decades, extensive research has been conducted about the identification of personality types (Hartman, 1999; Myers, 1995; Keirsey & Bates, 1984; Pascal, 1992). Regardless of which personality type index one chooses to examine and use, every personality has a specific way that it expresses and manages itself, particularly in times of stress. Knowledge of personality types enables us to be prepared for behaviors generally associated with the specific types, including our own.

It would be very convenient for us if we could interact only with the types of personalities we find the easiest and most enjoyable to connect with. The reality is that we will encounter people we interact very well with and some we do not interact with as well. The latter type of interactions can be mentally and emotionally stressful. We must also know which personality types "push our buttons" so that we are able to respond, rather than react, to people who demonstrate behaviors that can activate our mental and emotional triggers. When interacting with varying personalities, we must also be able to identify our own personality tendencies. This awareness informs us about which types of personalities are in concert, and in conflict, with our own. With this information, we can better manage ourselves when faced with the behaviors of individuals who demonstrate the traits that are most difficult for us to accept.

The four types of personalities considered here are the aggressive personality, passive-aggressive personality, withdrawn/depressed personality, and dependent personality. These types and their descriptions refer, in particular, to how a specific personality handles stress and conflict. Although all of us can demonstrate any of these behaviors at any time, when challenged, there is usually a more comfortable place each of us will naturally occupy. It is the examination of these behaviors and tendencies that can assist us in identifying ourselves among these four types. In Long, Morse, Fescer, and Newman's (2007) *Conflict in the Classroom* and Starr Commonwealth's (2001) *Building Safe and Reclaiming Schools,* the four personality types and the behaviors often demonstrated by each are detailed as follows.

Aggressive Personality

The aggressive personality exhibits the following in times of extreme conflict and stress:

- Angry, acting-out, threatening, and attacking behavior
- Behavior that often leads to power struggles
- Behavior that shows a loss or disabling of internal controls

- Behavior that often causes massive counteraggressive feelings in others
- Behavioral expressions of being overwhelmed, flooded, and consumed by feelings
- Behaviors that often force others to operate on the edge of learned skills, practiced competence, and personal levels of tolerance and patience
- Behaviors that often cause others to react rather than respond

Characteristics of the aggressive personality can include the following:

- The aggressive personality's anger can be triggered by altered states induced by alcohol, drugs, sleep deprivation, or stress. These factors distort the ability to perceive reality accurately and can lead to acts of aggression.
- The aggressive personality is challenged when required to tolerate a normal amount of personal frustration, disappointment, and anxiety.
- The aggressive personality often does not own his or her angry feelings but rather is flooded and overwhelmed by them. The aggressive personality projects feelings by depreciating or attacking others.
- The aggressive personality frequently expresses a loss of self-control or a sudden impulse breakthrough.
- The aggressive personality can be triggered by the need for stimulation or acknowledgment, not realizing that he or she can be acknowledged for appropriate behavior (i.e., the individual is demonstrating what he or she knows and is comfortable with).
- The aggressive personality's angry feelings and behavior can be triggered by his or her need to maintain status and role in the group.
- The aggressive personality often fears closeness and trusts no one; the aggressive behavior serves the individual by

pushing others away and minimizing the opportunity for the person to be hurt or rejected.

- Aggressive individuals who have been abused, abandoned, and deprived often seek punishment because they have been led to believe that their mistreatment is their fault; the aggressive behavior pushes others to punish them, which in turn reinforces the individual's belief that he or she is "bad."

- The aggressive personality often uses acting-out behavior to mask depression and sadness, thereby using aggression as a psychological and behavioral defense against uncomfortable feelings.

- An aggressive personality is often developed and stimulated by an overexposure to violent acts, including those portrayed in the media and those the person actually witnesses. Such exposure can lead to impulsive and aggressive behavior.

Passive-Aggressive Personality

The passive-aggressive personality uses the following behaviors to respond to extreme conflict and stress:

- Learned behaviors that include subtle expressions of anger toward others, often in irritating and indirect ways

- Emotional concealment, characterized by hiding anger behind annoying and confusing behaviors

- Behaviors that are often difficult to manage because they can provoke a great deal of frustration in others

- A combination of passive behavior and aggressive thoughts and feelings into one behavior (e.g., the person might think, "I'm very angry at you, but I'll smile and say I'm fine and plan to get you back later")

- A variety of behaviors designed to get back at another person without that person's recognizing the underlying anger

- Behaviors that are damaging and destructive to interpersonal relationships

- Behaviors that, as part of a long-lasting pattern, can become covert and insidious

Characteristics of the passive-aggressive personality include the following:

- The passive-aggressive personality's behavior is motivated by fear of expressing anger directly. The individual believes that the answer is to express anger indirectly.

- The passive-aggressive personality is often evasive and secretive. He or she does not talk about personal feelings and experiences easily. The passive-aggressive personality is manipulative, controlling, and often does not tell the truth about situations or his or her involvement in them.

- The expression of passive-aggressive behavior often creates feelings of confusion and frustration in those who are subjected to the behavior; it feels as though they are on an emotional roller coaster. The ups and downs of emotions in reaction to this personality can be quite intense and draining.

- The passive-aggressive personality always wishes to appear calm. Therefore, he or she can create great feelings of guilt in others who find themselves angry at the passive-aggressive individual. The receivers of passive-aggressive behavior often "swallow" their feelings of anger but later can explode in major ways.

- The passive-aggressive personality denies feelings of anger. These feelings have become dangerous or unacceptable for this personality. Consequently, the denial of angry feelings is motivated by the fear of expressing such feelings.

- The passive-aggressive personality sends hidden, coded, and confusing messages to others when frustrated or confronted.

- The passive-aggressive personality is very skilled at creating minor, but chronic, feelings of frustration and irritation in others, while appearing to be calm and harmless.

- The passive-aggressive personality is generally socially cooperative with others.
- One of the primary strategies that the passive-aggressive personality will use to express anger passively is procrastination or the inefficient completion of assigned tasks.

Generally, the passive-aggressive personality can be categorized into Type I and Type II. The Type I passive-aggressive personality has learned behavioral responses as a reaction to early, extended, and excessive physical and psychological abuse by parents. These individuals have learned that the expression of anger is dangerous as a result of the abuse they have suffered. This personality believes that while they may not be able to express anger directly because they will be hurt, they can get back at those who hurt them through hostile thoughts and passive actions. Intelligence is used to frustrate those they feel anger toward.

The Type II passive-aggressive personality is developed as a reaction to early, extended, and excessive parental expectations regarding goodness and guilt. These individuals learn to express anger through the excessive use of defenses such as blaming, projecting, or holding the anger inside of themselves. This often causes physical symptoms that arise at times of anger or frustration. These individuals have learned that the expression of anger is unacceptable and inappropriate for "good" people. The Type II personality is also often behaviorally motivated by intense feelings of guilt whenever feelings of anger or frustration arise.

Withdrawn/Depressed Personality

Personalities who tend to withdraw and become depressed can exhibit a number of distinctive behaviors:

- Sadness that may last a few hours to a few days due to minor disappointments, frustrations, fatigue, and the like.
- Behaviors that are in reaction to a specific external life event that is extremely meaningful to the individual, such as a

death, divorce, illness, a move, unexpected changes, and similar occurrences. Generally, this type of situational depression lasts from a few weeks to several months and can be healed, over time, with minimal professional intervention.

- Behaviors developed as an outcome of medical illness, including chronic illness, major surgery, and substance abuse (i.e., secondary behaviors).

- Behaviors and an emotional state that are clinical in nature and that differ from other states of depression in that they occur without a preexisting condition. Such primary depression often lasts from six months to one or two years, includes specific physical symptoms, and generally requires medication. Behaviors that indicate the most serious state of depression seem to occur without any obvious external cause and generally evidence themselves very quickly. The inner reality of the individual is its source, and often the individual is at risk for suicide.

Characteristics of individuals with a withdrawn/depressed personality type may include the following:

- These individuals have internalized negative ways of thinking about themselves, their world, and their circumstances. These negative ways of thinking motivate and further solidify their irrational thought patterns.

- Negative internal self-talk triggers further feelings of guilt, pessimism, sadness, and worthlessness. In turn, these anxiety-producing thoughts drive these individuals' inappropriate behaviors, including a general lack of interest in the world, activities, and possessions; withdrawal from social settings; isolation from others; and a general expression of wanting to be alone.

- Withdrawn/depressed individuals can become infatuated with their own "dark worlds" and drawn to negative thoughts. These behaviors are evidenced by the depressed personality as a "turning inward" on oneself.

- The withdrawn/depressed personality can often be quite agreeable. These individuals generally are not disruptive and do not cause major crisis events.

- Often the characteristics of the withdrawn/depressed personality are quite subtle, particularly at the onset of the period of depression.

- Withdrawn/depressed individuals can create a "mask" covering their deep depression. In some cases, the mask is one of defiance, anger, and rejection of assistance from others. In this case, these individuals are protecting themselves from further hurt, pain, and depressed feelings.

- These individuals often communicate feelings of hopelessness, worthlessness, and intense sadness. During these times, they may begin patterns of suicidal ideation and/or actions.

Dependent Personality

Personalities that are characterized by dependent behavior in times of stress and conflict can express the following:

- Behavior that is often learned and demonstrated in entire family systems and is often present in excessively tight-knit or enmeshed families

- Behavior due to anxieties about being left alone or abandoned

- Behavior that is extremely overwhelming to other people involved in personal relationships with these individuals

- Behavior that may be the result of an excessive need to please and be close to others

- Behavior that greatly limits independent activity, the ability to manage change, and normal emotional development

- Behavior that may develop after the loss of a significant person (parent, relative, friend, etc.) or dramatic changes in life circumstances, such as constant moving, dramatic inconsistencies in caretaking, and the like

- Behavior that expresses a self-perception of being unable to function independently and without the constant assistance of others
- Behavior that is extremely challenging for others because these individuals allow and expect others to take care of them and take responsibility for their lives

The dependent personality can be characterized in the following ways:

- The dependent personality may experience excessive anxiety about separating from home or from specific people.
- The dependent personality may have significant issues or impairment in social and intellectual functioning. These individuals are often social loners and may prefer to be in the company of others they feel comfortable with or protected by.
- Individuals with this personality type are often preoccupied with a fear of what will happen to them or to those to whom they are attached.
- Dependent individuals experience a lack of comfort in being away from home or from others to whom they are attached. They often appear phobic and may refuse to attend normal activities that require them to be away from home or significant others.
- Individuals with a dependent personality type are often unable to be decisive about simple or relatively minor things (e.g., what social activities to engage in, what color to wear, what to eat for lunch).
- The dependent personality may refuse to participate in normal activities independently.
- The dependent personality will often be excessively "clingy," both physically and emotionally. This behavior is beyond the normal attachment to significant others and becomes a source of intrusion for others.

- The dependent personality often exhibits excessive social withdrawal, sadness, or difficulty concentrating on ordinary tasks such as work and recreational activities.

The dependent personality demands constant attention and can be intrusive to others. In summary, Tool 1, Awareness and Management of Self, asks us to be willing to take an honest and in-depth look at ourselves, our behaviors, and how we present ourselves to others. It also asks us to take responsibility for what this examination reveals to us and to manage what we discover. In 1955, over half a century ago, Jersild wrote:

> To help a [child] have meaningful experiences, an [adult] must know the [child] as a person. This means that the [adult] must strive to know himself. An [adult's] understanding of others can be only as deep as the wisdom he possesses when he looks inward upon himself. How does one achieve understanding of self? One broad principle is this: to gain knowledge of self, one must have the courage to seek it and the humility to accept what one may find. (pp. 82–83)

Tool 1, then, asks us to do what we frequently ask children to do—be honest about ourselves, take responsibility for ourselves, and change what we determine must be changed.

3

We cannot expect more of our students than we expect of ourselves. We must act the way we expect our students to behave. If we want to work effectively with difficult students, we must be willing to change ourselves. Although we rarely appreciate our most difficult students because of the time they take and the frustration they cause, their presence can lead to growth if we learn from the obstacles they throw in our way.

—Allen Mendler and Richard Curwin (1999)

Tool 2: Knowledge of the Dynamics of Conflict

Recent research suggests that many of the crises taking place in school settings are either created or exacerbated by the adults in the setting and by the punitive and harsh policies adults develop and enforce there (Brendtro, Ness, & Mitchell, 2001; Long, Wood, & Fecser, 2001; Seita & Brendtro, 2002). This finding speaks to the level of conflict experienced by and between adults and children. Given that adults are charged with helping things get better, not making things get worse, why is this occurrence so prevalent in schools, in families, and in communities? Tool 2, Knowledge of the Dynamics of Conflict, helps us answer this question.

DISSECTING THE DYNAMICS OF CONFLICT

Understanding the nature of conflict requires a close examination of crisis events and three critical truths about conflict. These truths support us in understanding the dynamics involved in conflict and how we participate in this dynamic. These truths are (a) that we must respond more and react less, (b) that relief from a crisis is not the same as resolution of a crisis, and (c) that conflict is not equivalent to crisis.

Truth 1: We must respond more and react less

In order for us to respond more and react less, we must first understand the basis of responding and reacting. Responding is based on cognition, or logical thought. When we are able to respond to children in conflict, we are using logical and rational thinking to offer a response that is helpful to the situation.

37

Conversely, reacting is based on our emotions. When we are reacting to children in conflict, our emotions are leading us. When we are being led by emotions, we often interact with children in ways that escalate, rather than de-escalate, conflict. Using the skill of de-escalation helps us to avoid power struggles and respond to conflict rather than react in ways that make situations worse for ourselves and for children.

Truth 2: Relief from a crisis is not the same as resolution of a crisis

In a conflict, it is normal for us to want relief from the situation. As human beings, when we are faced with conflict or anxiety, it is natural for us to take flight or to fight. When faced with a child in conflict, we often confuse relief with resolution. When the child is removed from our immediate environment or receives a consequence for his or her behaviors, we have been relieved of the immediate situation. However, we often fool ourselves by telling ourselves that the situation has been resolved. Although we have been relieved of the immediate situation and, in some cases, of having to interact with the child, we have not necessarily resolved anything. Glasser (1998c) explains the idea of relief versus resolution as follows: "Kicking disruptive students out of class, keeping them after school in detention, or suspending them may control the immediate situation, but it does not deal with the basic problem" (p. 137). Resolution requires active participation in a process with the child that supports the child in (a) learning new self-supportive behaviors and (b) trying positive behaviors in times of future conflict.

Truth 3: Conflict and crisis are not the same thing

This truth is very important for us to remember when we are interacting with children in conflict. We would like to create a world for ourselves and our children that does not include conflict or anxiety. Unfortunately, this is not possible, and conflict is bound to occur at some point. However, the presence of conflict does not necessarily mean that a crisis must take place. Once we examine the Conflict Cycle, we will learn that we can respond in ways that manage and de-escalate conflict and that support coping behaviors in children. Responding is our alternative to reacting in ways that create crisis events and reinforce acting-out behaviors in children. When crisis events do occur—and they will—it is important for us to be able to learn from crisis events. According to an ancient Chinese saying, "Crisis is opportunity." The question is "An opportunity for what?" We can ensure that the answer for our children is "Crisis is an opportunity for learning!"

THE CONFLICT CYCLE: A PARADIGM FOR UNDERSTANDING

The Conflict Cycle (see Figure 4) is a paradigm that assists us in understanding the component parts of conflict (Long, 2007). In addition, the Conflict Cycle model teaches us that each of us has a self-concept and frame of reference that serve as unconscious filters for all information we receive and all events we experience. This self-concept and its frame of reference have a powerful impact on children, particularly in times of conflict. These filters will greatly determine how children will perceive, think, and feel about their life events and what they believe about themselves and the adults in their environment. Because children are often under stress, the patterns of their thoughts and feelings can become rigid and illogical, depending on their beliefs about the events of their lives. These patterns can limit and restrict their ability to create positive future outcomes.

The way that we handle conflict will determine whether a crisis event occurs. If we do not handle conflict effectively, it can, and often does, escalate into crisis (see Figure 5). By using Tool 2, we acquire critical information that can guide us in responding

FIGURE 4
The Conflict Cycle

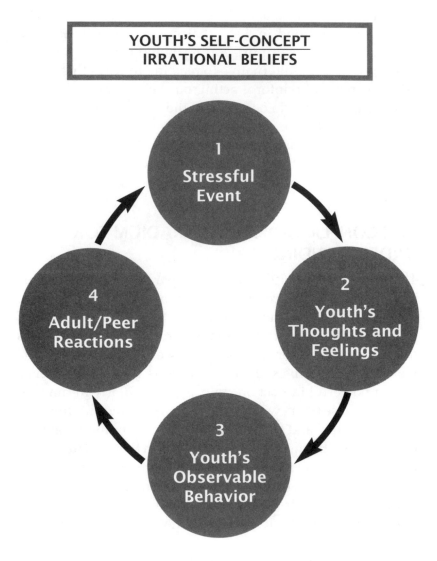

YOUTH'S SELF-CONCEPT
IRRATIONAL BELIEFS

1
Stressful
Event

2
Youth's
Thoughts and
Feelings

3
Youth's
Observable
Behavior

4
Adult/Peer
Reactions

rather than reacting to conflict, resolving conflict with children, and addressing conflict in ways that do not create harmful crisis events. The knowledge embedded in this tool reminds us of the following:

- Everyone, including adults, has a self-concept and frame of reference that serve as a filter for seeing and understanding the world.

- We all have choices in how we manage our personal feelings. In order to help our children manage their feelings and make self-supportive choices, we must be able to manage our own personal feelings.

- If we are unaware of our own emotions, triggers, and behaviors, we run the risk of mirroring the acting-out behavior of children in times of crisis.

- In power struggles, no one wins. We may be relieved of the situation, but the children we seek to help may pay the price for our inability to facilitate resolution of the crisis.

- Conflict occurs in a predictable and patterned sequence of stress, thoughts, feelings, behavior, and environmental reactions.

- Patterns of acting-out behavior on the part of children and adults create movement through multiple revolutions of conflict, resulting in major crisis incidents for both.

- Breaking the Conflict Cycle that takes place for adults and children is possible and is the responsibility of the adults in the environment. In order to interrupt this patterned and habitual response to conflict, adults must first monitor and address their own feelings.

Long (2007) presents the sequence of the Conflict Cycle by describing a series of events that take place when adults are trapped in conflict with children and youth. This paradigm also asks us to consider that adults often inadvertently create power struggles for themselves and youth that reinforce children's self-perceptions and decisions, although unconscious, to continue behaving in ways that are self-defeating.

The Conflict Cycle progresses through the following six steps:

1. A stressful event occurs for the child that prompts irrational thoughts and beliefs (e.g., "Nothing good ever happens to me!" or "Adults won't help me!").
2. The child's negative thoughts and feelings affect and interact with each other.
3. These thoughts and feelings prompt and drive the child's inappropriate behavior.
4. The child's inappropriate behavior angers adults in the environment and prompts their thoughts, feelings, and behavior.
5. Adults begin to feel the feelings of the child and frequently mirror the behaviors of the child.
6. The negative adult reaction increases the child's stress and escalates the conflict into a power struggle between the child and adult.

Once this struggle begins and escalates, several things happen:

- The child's motivation for changing behavior greatly decreases because the struggle reinforces the child's self-perceptions and beliefs about others.
- The child begins to believe that his or her thoughts, feelings, and behaviors are justified, increasing the likelihood for the behavior's reoccurrence.
- The adult may find this cycle with a particular child occurring more often and can begin to react to his or her own irrational thoughts and feelings with more frequency, intensity, and duration.

STRESS AND CONFLICT

Understanding the role that stress plays in the occurrence of conflict is important in our efforts to decrease crisis events for ourselves and children. Stress is defined as a personal and

FIGURE 5
Conflict into Crisis

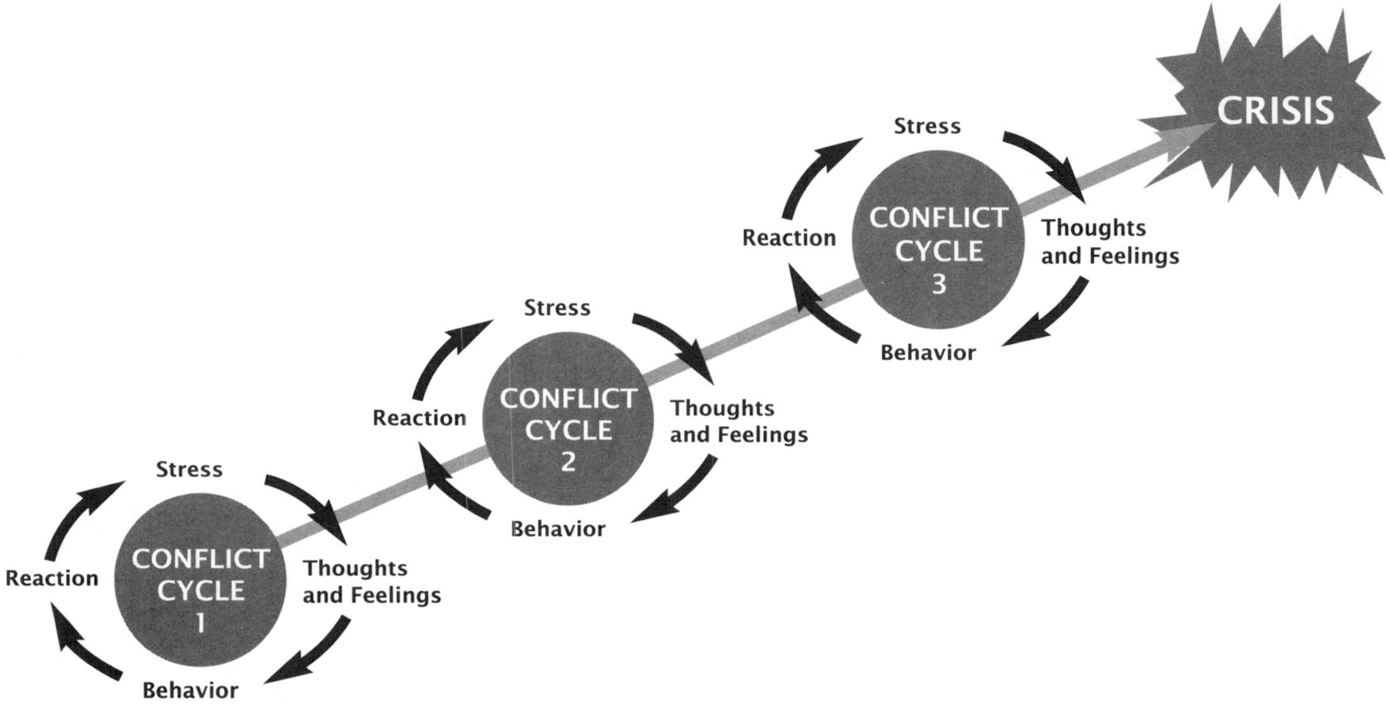

CRISIS
CONFLICT CYCLE 1
Stress
Thoughts and Feelings
Behavior
Reaction
CONFLICT CYCLE 2
Stress
Thoughts and Feelings
Behavior
Reaction
CONFLICT CYCLE 3
Stress
Thoughts and Feelings
Behavior
Reaction

subjective reaction to a specific life event, meaning that what creates stress for one person may not create stress for another. Stress is the reaction to the experience of physiological and psychological feelings of discomfort. Although stress can be useful in our lives by keeping us safe or motivating us to act, its usefulness depends on the degree of its frequency, intensity, and duration.

Stress can also be categorized (Long, Fecser, & Brendtro, 1998). Generally, stress can originate from four specific sources: developmental, economic/physical, psychological, and reality. The first type, developmental stress, is stress that arises from all the normal developmental crises or stages from birth to death. These developmental events are both stressful and predictable.

Economic/physical stress is a type of stress being increasingly experienced by many adults and children. Economic stress shows itself in the results of poverty, joblessness, and inability to maintain oneself financially. Physical stress may be evidenced by lack of sleep, physical exhaustion, and poor habits relating to diet and other aspects of health.

Psychological stress results from deep worry concerning issues and situations present in the life of an individual. Examples include family issues, relationship problems, abuse and neglect, or concerns about one's career or school placement.

Reality stress is generated by the unplanned events that impede the goals and plans of an individual. These are the events that we cannot anticipate or control and would prefer not to experience. Continued and frequent reality stress events can lead an individual to believe that the world and others are hostile and that his or her goals are being purposefully obstructed.

THOUGHTS, FEELINGS, AND CONFLICT

In understanding the dynamic of conflict, it is also helpful to consider how thoughts and feelings affect our ability to minimize the occurrence of conflict and crisis events. We already know that cognitive (thinking) and emotional (feeling) processes are in continuous interaction with one another. There is a circular, interacting relationship between thoughts and feelings. Cognitive experiences and emotional experiences affect each other simultaneously. Long (2007) describes this process in the following way:

> The process of thinking and feeling does not follow an independent path but is a continuous circular process. Thoughts trigger feelings, and negative feelings influence the way a person thinks about an event, creating a new cycle of negative feelings. (p. 338)

In other words, we think the way we feel and feel the way we think.

We often believe that our frustrations and anxieties are due exclusively to our feelings. What is truer is that our feelings and our thoughts affect our life events. The events do not create themselves; we have creative power over our life events through our thoughts and feelings. If we think and feel positively about an event, there is more opportunity for positive results. If we think and feel negatively about an event, more opportunity exists for negative results. Once we understand this concept, we can learn to respond to the events of our lives rather than constantly react to the things we perceive are happening to us.

We often unconsciously condition our thinking and feeling. When we experience the same event frequently and perceive this event as negative, we will eventually and automatically have negative thoughts and feelings about this event. When events that we perceive as similar to the "negative" event occur, we will also think and feel negatively about those events, even though they are not the same event. In this way, we restrict ourselves to a cycle that limits our thinking and feeling. This cycle is in continuous motion and interaction; in other words, it feeds on itself.

Once we begin to fully appreciate the power of our thoughts and feelings, we can comprehend how the quality of our thoughts and feelings can either predispose us to conflict or support us in avoiding crisis. This appreciation also supports us in managing our thoughts and feelings when conflict, stress, and crises do inevitably arise. Understanding our thoughts and feelings can also help us to examine an important question related to the dynamic of conflict: "Why do adults get angry at children and youth?"

ADULT ANGER AT CHILDREN AND YOUTH

There are many reasons adults find themselves filled with angry feelings and trapped by conflict that feeds on the anger. Otherwise reasonable adults can find themselves acting out their angry feelings in aggressive ways. When children become aggressive with us, we can become counteraggressive toward them when we react, as opposed to respond, to their behavior. Brendtro and du Toit (2005) discuss this phenomenon as the tit for tat rule: "Children in pain are likely to draw adults into escalating tit for tat hostility. The challenge is to prevent a vicious cycle where hate is answered with hate" (p. 7).

Awareness of feelings allows us to choose differently (i.e., respond rather than react) when these feelings arise. In understanding why conflict happens, it is important for us to know the reasons we become counteraggressive as a result of our anger. Following are some reasons to consider:

- We are trapped in the Conflict Cycle and do not know how to find a way out.

- The child's behavior represents a violation of our basic value and belief systems. These values are often middle-class values that many children do not hold or operate within. When a child violates what is important to us, we often become angry at both the behavior and the person. Our reaction is to lash out at the child who does not uphold our value system.

- Life is filled with many opportunities to be upset, angry, or even in crisis. When we find ourselves angry, sometimes the source is our own preoccupation with our thoughts, feelings, and life situation. We may be personally overwhelmed and more prone to acting on our anger on a particular day.

- The child's behavior taps into our own unfinished business, and we become angry at the child rather than accept and explore our own psychological issues.

- Embarrassment may be at the core of our angry feelings. When we do not meet our own expectations, it is possible that we may project our feelings of anxiety and anger onto the child we are interacting with rather than accepting and owning our feelings of discomfort and disappointment.

- Helplessness and hopelessness can lead to anger. When we find ourselves working harder and more intensely without achieving the progress we are looking for, the natural frustration of this experience can lead to helplessness and hopelessness. At times, these feelings can turn into anger toward the child for not understanding and benefiting from our hard work.

Preconceived notions about who a child is and what the child will and can do may also lead to angry feelings. When the child displays the behavior we expect, we then tell ourselves we are justified in feeling angry, which increases the likelihood that we will become angry again—perhaps with more intensity and frequency. Although we may prefer to deny it, the truth is, adults often make significant contributions to the onset and continuation of conflict. Becoming aware of these contributions can support us in choosing differently before we find ourselves involved in this cycle—or once we are engaged in these behaviors, in stopping ourselves from participating further.

Adult contributions to conflict may include the following:

- The use of "you-messages," described more fully later in this chapter (e.g., "Can't *you* do anything right?" or "*You* need to apologize to me immediately!" or "*You* need to stop that behavior right now!")

- The personalization of a child's behavior (e.g., "He directed that behavior at me personally!")

- Righteous indignation (e.g., "I have a right to be angry. After all, I am the adult and the one who helped that child before!")

- The refusal to remove the ego from interactions with children in crisis (e.g., "My pride is wounded, and I need to defend myself!")

- The placing of adult needs before the needs of children (e.g., "This is what I need from this situation in order to be OK!")

- The exertion of power and control issues with children in crisis (e.g., "I'm going to show her who is in charge!")

- The belief that punishment will make long-lasting changes in behavior (e.g., "If I just find the right punishment and make it painful enough, he'll stop this behavior!")

- Reacting rather than responding to a crisis (e.g., "This behavior is making me mad, and it must stop immediately at all costs!")

- Refusal to accept, own, or alter personal acting-out behavior (e.g., "It's all right for me to yell and threaten this child. I'm the adult! I can do what I want to do!")

THE SKILL OF DE-ESCALATION

Once we become knowledgeable about how conflict begins and escalates, the next step in understanding the dynamic of conflict is to learn how we can intervene effectively in the behavioral incidents that lead to conflict and crisis. One of the most effective and necessary skills we must master is the skill of de-escalation.

The use of de-escalation enables us as adults to (a) manage ourselves appropriately in times of conflict and during crisis events; (b) manage the acting-out and aggressive behavior of children; and (c) intervene with youth in ways that are helpful, not harmful. In times of conflict involving children, the following six techniques allow us to de-escalate potential harmful situations and avoid their escalating into crisis events:

Technique 1: Establish and Maintain Your Emotional Equilibrium

- Stay centered and calm.
- Remind yourself of your role as a helping adult.

- Do not let the emotional and behavioral instability of the child upset your emotional and behavioral stability.
- Appear calm and controlled.
- Avoid the urge to shout, point a finger, threaten, or insult the child; these behaviors will generally prompt the child to engage in more defensive and attacking behaviors toward you.

Technique 2: Understand the Child's Point of View

- Attempt to put yourself in the child's psychological shoes.
- Appreciate the child's perspective; try to be empathic and attentive to how the child is feeling about and perceiving the situation.

Technique 3: Focus on the Child's Needs

- Tune in to the child's needs.
- Understand that when the child feels that his or her needs are not being met, the child can become more defensive, guarded, and combative.

Technique 4: Set the Intention of Resolving the Conflict or Crisis

- Be willing to open the door toward resolution; in most cases, the child wants to resolve the situation as much as you do.
- Offer the child a way out of the situation while allowing the child to retain his or her dignity (i.e., to "save face"); avoid backing the child into a corner, either physically or psychologically, so the child will not feel the need to fight his or her way out.

Technique 5: Monitor and Control Your Body Language

- Children and youth are very aware of the behaviors they perceive from others, particularly those that they find threatening. Manage your facial expressions, tone of voice, and body language; these are important indicators of your level of control.

- Avoid standing face-to-face with an aggressive child—this can be perceived as a direct physical threat.

- Have an open body posture, with hands by your sides in a relaxed position.

- Show your hands at all times so the child does not perceive that you may be hiding an object that can be used as a weapon.

- Try to maintain your composure and verbally assure the child that your agenda is to resolve the difficulty, not to create a confrontational or aggressive situation.

Technique 6: Be Responsible for the Outcome

- Accept your responsibility for your contribution to the conflict situation; if it is appropriate for you to apologize for your behavior, be a positive role model and do so.

- Communicate your responsibility for the outcome; by doing so, you make it easier for the child to accept and admit his or her responsibility for the situation.

- Make it clear to the child that resolving the crisis situation requires the effort of both of you.

I-MESSAGES VERSUS YOU-MESSAGES

Language also plays a critical role in the dynamic of conflict. How we speak to a child in times of conflict and crisis can make the difference between the escalation of conflict or the resolution of conflict. One of the ways we can use language to effectively manage conflict is to use I-messages instead of you-messages.

I-messages are statements that focus on you instead of the other person. These statements can help avoid the escalation of conflict because they accomplish the following:

- Shift the attention away from the person in conflict

- Make your wishes and requests known without ordering the other person to do something
- Communicate your willingness to support the other person in demonstrating more functional behavior
- De-escalate your behavior by enabling you to verbalize what you are observing and feeling

In contrast, you-messages are messages that focus on the other person. They encourage escalation of conflict and increase the likelihood of crisis because they can result in the following negative consequences:

- Blaming the other person for doing something unacceptable
- Identifying the other person as the "problem" or as "wrong"
- Creating the need for the other person to defend himself or herself
- Threatening and attacking the other person

Following are some examples of you-messages:

"You never do anything right!"

"You are always breaking the rules!"

"You think everything is about making you happy, don't you?"

Now, how can we transform the same you-messages into I-messages? Some possibilities are provided here:

"I see you are having some trouble with that. Can I help you?"

"I'm wondering if you're aware that we have a rule about that? Can I tell you what that rule is?"

"I feel like something is not going well here. Can we talk about what we can do differently?"

A simple shift in how we speak and on whom we focus can make the difference between a conflict that escalates into crisis and a conflict that reaches resolution.

SUGGESTIONS FOR AVOIDING THE OCCURRENCE AND ESCALATION OF CONFLICT

Understanding the dynamics of conflict not only requires that we learn what to look for when conflict is present, it also asks that we consider what we can do to prevent conflict and crisis from occurring. The following tips can help us avoid creating conflict for ourselves and others:

- Stay in touch with your own feelings.
- Safeguard yourself from "catching" and acting on the feelings of others.
- Openly verbalize your feelings. It is healthy for us to be able to speak about our feelings, and it provides a model for children who have difficulty speaking about theirs.
- Model coping strategies that can help children learn how to manage difficult situations before they escalate. By doing this, you can also help them decrease personal stress and encourage your own feelings of competence and success.
- Make a conscious decision *not* to engage in power struggles with children.
- Use the skill of de-escalation to focus on resolution, as opposed to becoming lost in feelings and behavior.
- Use language to support the resolution of conflict. In other words, use I-messages rather than you-messages.
- Focus on what children need instead of on what you are feeling.
- Help children identify coping strategies that work for them.
- Support children when they accept personal responsibility for their actions by accepting and modeling the same type of responsibility.
- Support and accept feelings (both yours and those of children) while insisting that feelings be managed by demonstrating acceptable behavior for the setting.

- Help children focus on their resiliency and ways in which they can develop a greater capacity for dealing with upset and disappointment.

To conclude, conflict is indeed an inevitable part of life, both for adults and for children. Tool 2 asks us to be aware of how and why conflict is created and then to practice effective management techniques that include preventing the escalation of conflict into crisis. This tool also asks us to embrace a deeper understanding of conflict by considering the persons involved in the conflict. In understanding this dynamic, we also consider how the individual makeup of a person—in other words, his or her self-perception and frame of reference, along with the thoughts, feelings, and beliefs derived from these—contribute to the occurrence of conflict and the ease (or lack thereof) with which conflict is resolved.

4

Discipline programs can (temporarily) change behavior, but they cannot help people grow. The latter requires a very different orientation in the classroom: looking "through" a given action in order to understand the motives that gave rise to it as well as figuring out how to have some effect on those motives.

—Alfie Kohn (1996)

Tool 3: Understanding the Differences between Behavior Management and Behavior Change

I often visit schools that ask me to help them analyze the behavior of their students and the adult responses to that behavior. During those visits, I usually ask this question: "Is your school responding to behavior mostly by managing behavior, supporting change of behavior, or both?" Most school professionals say they are either changing behavior or are engaged in both managing and changing behavior. However, more often than not, the truth is that the school and the adults in the school are mostly using behavior management strategies.

When I asked myself why these well-seasoned professionals tell me the opposite of what is actually happening in their settings, it became very clear to me that they were not intentionally deceiving themselves or me. I eventually understood, through repeated conversations and observations, that the adults didn't know the differences between managing behavior and supporting the change of behavior.

Tool 3, Understanding the Differences between Behavior Management and Behavior Change, can be of great support to us in facilitating positive behavior because it provides clarity regarding our intentions in responding to the behavior of children and youth. Many of us are willing to address the behavior we see from the children we serve; however, we are often

55

unclear about what we are attempting to accomplish in addressing this behavior. Another critical question I ask adults is this: "When you respond to a child's behavior by doing or saying X, what do you expect to happen?" Again, many professionals answer my question with blank stares, "I don't know," or "I'm unsure." In some cases, they explain their expectations, seemingly without understanding that their responses are completely unaligned with their expectations. In one case, I received a particularly startling response from an adult who had entangled herself in a student's Conflict Cycle. When I asked the question about her expectations for the student's behavior, she responded with "When I yelled at him, I expected him to stop yelling at me!"

We must understand that making a decision about managing behavior or supporting change of behavior is critical in facilitating positive behavior. Once we make this decision, we must realize that behavior management requires us to use skills that are very different from skills we use to facilitate behavior change. In order to facilitate positive behavior, we must understand the differences between these two goals, be able to carry out both goals effectively, and be clear about when it is appropriate to manage behavior and when it is appropriate to facilitate change of behavior. (Appendix B describes a range of strategies and techniques for behavior management and behavior change.)

Many adults who are interacting with children and youth may be addressing behavior without fully understanding the skills they are using or why they are using particular skills. Programs are often ineffective in addressing children's challenging behavior because the adults involved have not stopped to ask what their goals are when intervening: management or support of change. Tool 3 encourages us to identify the continuum of skills (see Figure 6) that we can use and to be able to communicate with others regarding why we chose a particular intervention to address a specific behavior. Once we are clear about our intentions when intervening in behavior— management or change—we can begin to examine what is

FIGURE 6

A Continuum of Behavior Management and Behavior Change Techniques

BEHAVIOR MANAGEMENT

BEHAVIOR CHANGE

Surface Behavior Management
Techniques (SBMT's)
Rewards and Consequences
Discipline Systems/Rules
Codes of Conduct

Class Meetings
Contracting
Student Conferencing
Token Economies
Level Systems
Point Systems
Therapeutic Crisis Intervention
(TCI)

Life Space Crisis Intervention
(LSCI)
Student Interviews
Therapeutic Milieu/Groupings

necessary from us in each instance. In this way, when we intervene in behavior, we can choose the skills and techniques most appropriate for meeting our goals.

MANAGING BEHAVIOR

It is generally easier for adults to manage the surface behavior—or the behavior that is visible and obvious—of children and youth. However, the behavior will often return because the children displaying the behavior have not learned to do anything new. In other words, no real change has taken place. Imagine this scenario: You spend all day with the children in your care, addressing their behavior. You work very hard to ensure that children are well-behaved and are doing their best. By the end of the day, you are drained and weary from running from child to child, addressing their behavior! You go home at the end of the day and barely have enough energy for the things you would like to do. Tomorrow, when you return to the children, they demonstrate the exact same behavior you spent all day addressing yesterday! Days like this turn into weeks and months and, before you know it, perhaps even a year has gone by! In a quandary, you ask yourself: "What is going wrong?!"

If this situation sounds familiar, you may be caught in what is called the "firefighter role." You spend a great deal of your energy putting out fires and making sure that no one gets hurt, but nothing ever really changes for the children in your care. In this case, you may be trapped in managing the behavior of the children, unable to move them along the continuum toward real behavior change.

A challenge we face is the overuse—or exclusive use—of behavior management systems. These systems can initially address acting-out behavior effectively; however, after some time, the rewards offered to children become meaningless, and the acting-out behaviors return. In these instances, both behavior management techniques and behavior change strategies must be used in order for children to grow and adopt new behavioral patterns. Once we are able to use both methods for addressing behavior, we can make decisions regarding the strategies we will use to best respond to the scenario, the child's needs, and the child's developmental and emotional levels.

It is true that some children need external rewards to manage their difficult behaviors. However, our children are better served when we assist them in learning how to respond to internal motivation instead of external motivation. Because we know that the world does not automatically reward us for doing the right thing, children must be taught that demonstrating positive behavior allows them to get their personal needs met in ways that are self-supportive.

SUPPORTING CHANGE IN BEHAVIOR

When a decision is made to facilitate behavior change in children and youth, we are required to form meaningful relationships and become involved with them. In other words, we are required to enter into their "life space." Entering into the life space of a child does not mean that we take personal responsibility for a child or become involved in ways that make us uncomfortable. However, this decision does require willingness to see ourselves as more than the titles we have been given and to support children in ways that encourage them in learning and living. We must also embrace another simple truth when deciding how to facilitate change in a child's behavior: We cannot change the behavior of another human being. Glasser (1998c) states this truth in the affirmative: "The only person any of us can consistently control is ourselves" (p. 75). This reality can be especially challenging for us as adults to accept. We often fool ourselves into believing that we are single-handedly saving, controlling, and changing children.

What we *can* do to facilitate the change of another's behavior is to develop relationships and create environments that support the other in deciding to change and control his or her own behavior. Once a child has made the decision to change a behavior, we can support that change by reminding him or her of the benefits of the change and by providing encouragement when the inevitable challenges generally associated with changing one's own behavior surface.

DIFFERENCES BETWEEN MANAGING BEHAVIOR AND FACILITATING BEHAVIOR CHANGE

As we become more knowledgeable about the differences between behavior management and methods of behavior change, we can begin to use the two more effectively when we intervene in a child's behavior.

Characteristics of Behavior Management

Specifically, behavior management involves the following:

- *Consciousness:* When behavior management techniques are being used, the child being managed is aware, or conscious, that an attempt is being made to manage his or her behavior, whether the attempt is successful or unsuccessful.

- *External/extrinsic methods:* The strategy of behavior management is external or extrinsic to the child who is being managed. In other words, the attempts to manage the behavior are being applied from outside sources—for instance, tangible reinforcements an adult might use to reward the child's behavior.

- *Addressing behavior:* Behavior management techniques address or speak to behavior. These techniques identify behaviors to be managed and/or confronted.

- *Regulation of behavior:* Behavior management attempts to regulate or influence the behavior of the child. These techniques attempt to control the behavior and may lead to the temporary termination of certain behaviors.

- *Specific identification of behaviors:* Behavior management techniques identify specific behaviors to be addressed and managed. When using behavior management techniques, the adult identifies a certain behavior as being inappropriate and brings it to the attention of the child, directly or indirectly.

- *Ease of use:* Initially, behavior management is easier for the adult because it does not necessarily require the adult to be in a relationship with the child being managed.

- *Temporary behavioral improvements:* Attempts to manage behavior are often temporary. Quite often, once the object of management being used is removed, the behavior returns.

- *Motivation of others:* The use of behavior management techniques is generally motivated by someone other than the person whose behavior is being managed. Usually, behavior management techniques are employed when the adult determines that a child is demonstrating a behavior that must be addressed and controlled.

Characteristics of Behavior Change

In contrast, support of behavior change involves the following:

- *The subconscious:* When the adult is facilitating behavior change, he or she may support a child's behavioral change on a subconscious or unconscious level. In other words, the child may not be consciously aware that the adult is attempting to facilitate change of a particular behavior.

- *Internal/intrinsic methods:* Behavior change is internal or extrinsic to the child. In other words, the child must make an internal decision to change the behaviors.

- *Resolving behavior:* At its best, behavior change techniques help resolve or explain behavior that is self-defeating for the child so it can be changed.

- *Eradication of behavior:* The ultimate goal of behavior change strategies is to eradicate or eliminate self-defeating behavior.

- *Generalized identification of undesirable behaviors:* Behavior change strategies are more general than behavior management techniques. At their best, behavior change strategies can be learned and applied to other behaviors that can be changed.

- *More challenging to use:* Initially, the use of behavior change strategies is more challenging for adults because the adults must be willing to form a genuine relationship with the child. In other words, they must be willing to enter into the child's life space in order to support change of behavior.

- *Permanency:* At their best, behavior change strategies make long-lasting changes in behavior.

- *Self-motivation:* The decision to change behavior must be motivated by the child—not by the adult who wants the child to demonstrate different behaviors.

In summary, using Tool 3 enables us to (a) gain clarity about our intentions in intervening in behavior, (b) choose the appropriate techniques based on our objectives, (c) begin to master the skills necessary to manage behavior and facilitate change of behavior, and (d) intervene in behavior in ways that best meet the developmental and emotional needs of the child.

5

The word "environment" denotes some-thing more than surroundings which encompass an individual. [It] denotes the specific continuity of the surroundings with his own active tendencies. In brief, the environment consists of those conditions that promote or hinder, stimulate or inhibit, the characteristic activities of a living being.

—John Dewey (1944)

Tool 4: Healing Environment

The role of Tool 4, the Healing Environment, is vital in PBF. This tool relates directly to the climate in which children and youth are served. As we know, many of our children have been wounded and are in need of environments that will support, nurture, and, in some cases, heal them. In previous years, most believed that the children in need of such milieus were those identified as disturbed, abused, or disordered. However, because the circumstances and environments in which many children presently live are less than optimum, a healing environment is now necessary for many more than in previous years.

The establishment of an environment that considers a child's perceptions, thoughts, and feelings is crucial to facilitating positive behavior. Long et al. (2007) describe this environment in this way:

> A therapeutic classroom or school is one that offers a climate of care, protects students from physical and psychological danger, respects students as individuals, offers freedom from prejudice, and provides a responsive and stimulating environment. (p. 135)

The development of such surroundings requires us to remember that all things in an environment have an impact on the well-being of children. Some of these qualities are clearly visible, while others are not so obvious. When using Tool 4, we must be aware of the impact on children's functioning of all factors present in the environment.

PBF recognizes that the atmosphere of an environment has a tremendous impact on the behavior of children in that environment. Many children will behave in one way in a certain setting and in a completely different way in another setting. This is often due to the atmosphere or climate of the particular setting. For example, when in a safe environment, children behave in ways that show they feel protected, at ease, and secure. Long (1997) tells us that children need specific acts of kindness in order to grow: "Just as sunlight is the source of energy that maintains organic life, kindness is the source of energy that maintains and gives meaning to humanity. Without sunlight and kindness, neither organic nor compassionate life can exist on this planet" (p. 242).

The healing environment has a quality that, while intangible, supports a child's intellectual and psychological functioning and promotes positive behavior. However, if that same child is in an environment where he or she feels unsafe or is treated with unkindness, the behavior we see will be very different. The child will behave in ways that communicate concerns about harm, danger, and threat. When we begin to observe the actions of children and ask ourselves what we can do to facilitate positive behavior, the healing environment assists us in understanding the importance of the environment, both physical and psychological.

THERAPEUTIC MILIEU: A FOUNDATION FOR THE QUALITIES OF THE HEALING ENVIRONMENT

Redl (1959a) coined the term *therapeutic milieu* and posited that understanding what constitutes a supportive and nurturing environment in a controlled setting can aid in the design of school and community programs for all children. He identified 12 components of the therapeutic milieu that he believed could be used in a variety of settings for healing children and youth.

Using Redl's work as a practical foundation, PBF describes the healing environment as one characterized by the following qualities:

1. Positive relationships
2. Ordered physical surroundings

3. Guidelines for living and learning

4. Spirit of community and family

5. Meaningful experiences

6. Skilled and caring adults

7. Focus on service

8. Recognition and management of group dynamics

9. Structured time

10. Recognition and management of outside influences

11. Customs and ceremonies

12. Established emotional climate

Quality 1: Positive Relationships

Brendtro and Shahbazian (2004) write that "positive relationships have proven to be the foundation of success. Whatever the treatment or educational model, there is widespread recognition that relationships are a necessary precondition to effective intervention" (p. 91). In the healing environment, the relationships that exist between adults and children provide the opportunity for the creation of bonds that allow children to take advantage of what well-meaning adults offer them, including education, care, respect, and nurturance. The relationships that exist between the adults also matter in the healing environment. Children learn how to treat one another from watching the adults in their environment. In the healing environment, the adults are aware that they are the models for building relationships. They provide examples of interactions that foster trust, openness, and emotional safety.

Quality 2: Ordered Physical Surroundings

The condition of the physical surroundings in which children find themselves sends a very clear message about how the adults view the setting, themselves, and others in that setting. A physical environment that has a certain degree of order and warmth can support children in feeling more comfortable and can facilitate the learning process. In creating ordered physical surroundings, it is not necessary for everything in the setting to be expensive or perfect. However, the healing environment does display a level of care and structure relating to the physical surroundings. Children feel welcomed when the surroundings are kept as neat, clean, inviting, and organized as possible. In other words, the healing environment understands that the physical surroundings reflect the feelings and thoughts about who is being served in the space.

Quality 3: Guidelines for Living and Learning

Although it is a well-researched and well-established belief that adults should clearly express what is acceptable and expected from children, Kohn (1996) presents a slightly different viewpoint on the issue of behavioral expectations. He informs us that allowing children to have a voice in determining what they will accept and expect from themselves is vital in preparing them to take an active role in a democratic society. In creating a healing environment, children participate in determining what they would like to see happen in their environment in order for successful living and learning to take place. Adults in the setting may provide guidance and options in terms of what can facilitate maximal learning and living; however, in the healing environment, children have a voice in establishing and communicating guidelines for behavior. The goal for the healing environment is to ensure that guidelines for behavior are not solely restrictive but are conducive to growth and, in some cases, restorative of a child's positive sense of self.

Quality 4: Spirit of Community and Family

In each of the schools I was fortunate enough to manage during what I call my "principal years," I often looked and listened for signs that the school was functioning as a community or even as a family. Some of the signs that were very clear indicators of how we were doing with this quality included how the adults talked to and cared for the students and each other; how the students talked to and cared for the adults and each other; the level of participation we had from students, families, and the community at large in extracurricular events and programs; how well we took care of our "home" (i.e., the school building); to what degree everyone (adults and students) accepted responsibility for what took place in our home; and the resolution of any challenges that arose within the "family."

The healing environment understands that relationships are the foundation for everything. In environments that operate with the spirit of community and family, relationships are authentic, supportive, and respectful in nature. The healing environment fosters such relationships and sees them as the springboard for the development of community and family spirit.

Quality 5: Meaningful Experiences

In 1938, Dewey wrote: "Above all, [adults] should know how to utilize the surroundings that exist so as to extract from them all that they can contribute to building up experiences that are worthwhile" (p. 40). Sixty years later, Glasser (1998b) suggested that the behavior of youth is tied directly to meaningful experiences when he stated, "Discipline is only a problem when students are forced into classes where they do not experience satisfaction" (p. 13). In the healing environment, adults provide experiences that are meaningful and directly connected to children's lives. Carlsson-Paige (2001) writes: "When children are expected to complete tasks that are not geared to their understanding, they become confused, begin to feel inadequate, begin to doubt their own ability to make sense" (p. 22). When children do not understand the value of the experiences they are being provided, adults in the healing environment are able to support them in understanding how the experiences relate to living, both now and in the future. In the healing environment, adults are never engaged in creating activities that are for the purpose of filling time; experiences always support children in becoming sensitized to their own lives and in living successfully. As Glasser (1998c, 1998d) suggests, when students are able to connect the meaning and value of their experiences to their lives, challenging behavior decreases as positive behavior increases.

Quality 6: Skilled and Caring Adults

In the healing environment, two critical characteristics of the adults who are serving children and youth are skill and care. One without the other is not enough. Although it might seem obvious, adults who work best with children are those who truly care about them. In this environment, caring extends beyond the school or program walls; the adults care about what happens to children when they are not in their presence, in children's homes, in their neighborhoods, and in their lives.

However, as we know, in serving today's children and youth, care alone is not enough. Not only must adults in the healing environment care for and about children, they must be skilled at what they do. One of the critical skills of caring adults is that of *with-it-ness* (Kounin, 1977). Kounin was the first to use this term to describe the adult's ability to know what is going on in the environment at all times. Although this term primarily describes teachers in classroom settings, the adult's level of with-it-ness in any healing environment can have a major impact on the behavior of youth. The level of comfort children have in believing that an adult truly does know what is taking place in the environment at all times influences their willingness to trust the environment and therefore depend on it for growth and support.

In the healing environment, the strengths of the adults are capitalized on, and adults are able to use their skills in the areas where they and children can be the most successful. In this environment, adults not only bring their unique gifts, the environment takes responsibility for developing and enhancing the skills of the adults. Regular and meaningful education is offered to help adults remain skilled in the areas that are most needed to support youth. The healing environment understands the importance of consistent and continual learning opportunities for adults in order to ensure the advancement of their skills.

Quality 7: Focus on Service

In collaboration with the Search Institute, Benson (1997) identified service to others as one of 40 positive experiences or qualities, labeled developmental assets, that have a significant and positive impact on the lives of children and youth. In *Waging Peace in Our Schools*, Lantieri and Patti (1998) espouse a new vision of education in which "porous boundaries" are created between schools and communities, largely by having students focus on how best to serve their communities. Further still, Brendtro and Larson (2006) tell us that in order "to nurture a sense of purpose, youth must be given opportunities to serve. . . . Youth must have some overall commitment to something beyond themselves" (pp. 132–133).

In the healing environment, adults and children understand the importance of serving each other, serving their immediate communities and families, and serving the community and world at large. Regular opportunities to serve are incorporated into the functioning of the healing environment. These can vary from in-house activities (e.g., painting rooms in the building) to those taking place outside of the environment (e.g., reading to younger children in the community). While practicing service, children can learn how to be compassionate, appreciative, and selfless—all of which support the demonstration of positive behavior in every arena of living (Brendtro & du Toit, 2005; Lickona, 2001, 2004).

Quality 8: Recognition and Management of Group Dynamics

The seminal writings *Controls from Within* (Redl & Wineman, 1952) and *Mental Hygiene in Teaching* (Redl & Wattenberg, 1959) offered the first explanations of group dynamics. These writings provided the field of education with the opportunity to understand how group behavior differs from individual behavior and set forth strategies for supporting adults in effectively managing the challenges of group behavior, particularly when that behavior is deemed undesirable. The healing environment understands that children are often susceptible to "group conta-gion," a dynamic that may cause them to behave in ways they would not normally behave when the group is not present. This is particularly true for adolescents, who are deeply concerned about the image they create and maintain within their peer group.

In the healing environment, the adults understand and effectively manage the psychological forces in groups that create pressure for individual children and youth. Groups have personalities, roles, standards, and rules. The healing environ-ment appreciates the uniqueness and interplay of these compo-nents when children come together in the environment and can assist them in effectively managing themselves (as individ-uals and as a group) while addressing the group forces at work.

Quality 9: Structured Time

Few would argue that when children are engaged in structured activities, the likelihood of their displaying challenging behav-iors decreases, while focused attention, motivation, and accept-able behaviors increase. Cushman (2003) reminds us that adults must be mindful not only of the types of activities we ask chil-dren and youth to be involved in, but also of the timing and the structure of those activities. Adults in the healing environment understand that when youth are presented with the opportu-nity to create their own agenda, they will do so. When we allow children to create a plan for themselves, we mustn't be surprised when that plan is not necessarily in alignment with what we would have planned.

The healing environment provides experiences structured with the needs of children and youth in mind, a strategy that Brendtro and Shahbazian (2004) call "structuring for success." Adults who consider how time is used in the healing environ-ment are able to strike the delicate balance between creating opportunities for children to learn how to manage themselves and their time and establishing boundaries around how time is used. Mand (1983) describes this balance: "[Adults] may have their own agendas of proposed programs, but the principal concern for the student is the activity, the skill and the . . . milieu" (p. 239). The healing environment understands that the concerns and needs of children must be a primary factor when deciding how to structure time.

Quality 10: Recognition and Management of Outside Influences

The healing environment understands that no matter how protected a setting may seem, it is not a vacuum. Adults in the milieu are responsible for supporting children in managing that which comes into the setting with them. In 1995, Goleman provided nonscientists with extremely meaningful information in his book *Emotional Intelligence.* In that work, the author explains the neuroscientific research that proves that what happens to an individual emotionally affects that individual's ability to perform, be present, and be successful. This is particularly true for children. When the outside world weighs heavily on children, as it does for many of today's youth, those influences follow them into any setting in which they find themselves. The healing environment recognizes the magnitude of those forces and supports children in managing the results of those forces, which are largely emotional.

Outside influences also enter into a setting through television, movies, and visitors, as well as through stories that children and adults tell each other. These influences can become a part of the setting and must be acknowledged by the adults who are creating a safe place for children. When these external factors are difficult for children to manage, adults in the healing environment step in to help them integrate these influences into their current experience. Adults also introduce other types of planned outside influences through trips and activities in the community.

In addition to considering planned influences, the healing environment is prepared for the numerous unplanned events that can take place and that have an impact on a setting. Families, communities, systems, and the world at large present any number of influences that can have an effect on and seep into an environment. The healing environment acknowledges the impact of these aspects on the milieu and accounts for them in its programmatic planning and implementation.

Quality 11: Customs and Ceremonies

In the healing environment, one of the ways a supportive culture is built is by establishing customs and ceremonies. Many of our children and youth exist in environments that are unpredictable and difficult at best. The nurturing setting values the importance of reliable routines and traditions. Nelsen, Lott, and Glenn (2000) tell us that customs that are predictable, consistent, and respectful to all can create long-term benefits for children, including feelings of security and stability, willingness to trust, and opportunities to practice responsibility and cooperation.

Ceremonies provide an opportunity for children and adults to acknowledge accomplishments. These ceremonies are organized by adults and children working together for the enjoyment and benefit of those in the setting. The opportunity to celebrate fosters personal confidence, closeness between those being celebrated and those celebrating, and the building of meaningful relationships. In the healing environment, ceremonies are a part of the established routine that children can depend on and look forward to. Celebration of individual children's accomplishments can also make them aware that they can be successful and are worthy of recognition.

Quality 12: Established Emotional Climate

Long (2000) tells us that one of the challenging but necessary elements in managing our individual personal feelings and behaviors is setting an emotional climate for ourselves and remaining at that "temperature," rather than allowing others to create a climate for us. The ability to establish and maintain an emotional climate is a necessary component of the healing environment. In the nurturing setting, a favorable climate is established, and the adults make every effort to maintain that temperature regardless of the influences that may attempt to increase or decrease it. Preservation of climate is particularly important when serving children and youth who live in emotionally unstable and unpredictable environments. When children are in erratic surroundings, much of their energy is spent on deflecting what may come their way and on navigating the emotionally rocky waters they may find themselves in, through no fault of their own. When children come to a place where they can count on a certain emotional atmosphere, they know what to expect, understand what is acceptable and unacceptable in that environment, and are able to relax and focus on the tasks the adults in the setting ask them to address.

PRACTICES OF THE HEALING ENVIRONMENT

The healing environment operates on the basis of a specific set of practices that guide the day-to-day functioning of the setting. When adults interact with children and each other with these practices in mind, the healing potential of the environment increases. These practices, briefly described in Table 3, provide the basis for establishing active and operational principles that can shape our work with children and youth. In addition, Appendix C includes a set of questions that support us in examining the presence of each practice within our healing environment. When asked and answered honestly, these questions can help us determine the degree to which of the practices are "real" in our surroundings. Used as guideposts for creating the healing environment, these questions can provide a framework for monitoring our ongoing efforts to operate with youth according to these practices.

PERSONALITIES AND THE HEALING ENVIRONMENT

Development of a healing environment requires that we address the individual needs of the children and youth in our care. As we learn to identify their personality traits, we can begin to structure the environment in ways that best address their mental, emotional, social, spiritual, and physical needs. Each personality type requires different therapeutic strategies for management and support. The suggestions below consider the personality types described in chapter 2 (aggressive, passive-

TABLE 3
Practices of the Healing Environment

Children as Thinkers

> Practice that moves children from having most of their decisions made by helping adults to becoming independent and responsible decision makers

Behavior as a Teaching Tool

> Practice that encompasses a structured and logical system of consequences in response to a child's behavior versus a focus on punishment in reaction to a child's behavior

The Whole Being

> Practice that considers the emotional and behavioral concerns of a child as well as the child's intellectual development and academic performance

Teaching about the Self

> Practice that assists children in developing insight into themselves and the motivations behind their behaviors

Why We Are Here

> Practice that recognizes the needs of children first

Everyone and Everything Matters

> Practice that considers all disciplines and helping adults equally necessary for children's success

The Three R's: Respect Received Reciprocally

> Practice that reflects a genuine respect for children

Relationships Are Everything

> Practice that recognizes that nurturing relationships between children and adults are critical to children's success in all domains

Happy Adults, Happy Children

Practice that acknowledges and supports the emotional health, wholeness, and well-being of the adults in order to offer the same to children

Every Child Can

Practice that demonstrates belief in the potential of all children, regardless of background, socioeconomic status, or familial history

---

aggressive, withdrawn/depressed, and dependent) and offer us specific techniques for meeting the unique needs of each type and addressing the behaviors each type displays.

Therapeutic Management of the Behavior of the Aggressive Personality

Since management of children and youth begins with us, the first step in addressing the behavior of the aggressive child is to control our own counteraggression. Strategies for managing counteraggression include substituting I-messages for you-messages, making a conscious decision not to fight with the child, thinking before acting, and focusing on the child's needs rather than on the child's behavior. The following suggestions are also helpful:

- Clearly and firmly state the positive behavior you expect the child to demonstrate. Make sure that your expectations are reasonable and can be accomplished by the child in that particular time, place, and situation.

- Accept the child's angry feelings but not his or her aggressive behavior. By monitoring our own feelings, we can ensure that we are not reacting to the child's behavior but are responding to his or her needs. We must accept the child and the child's feelings by ensuring that we do not lose sight of the fact that the child is an individual, not just the sum of his or her behavior.

- Refer to specific environment guidelines prohibiting this behavior. It is important that the child understand that the limits are not being placed on him or her alone but are general behavioral expectations for all children in the setting.

- Encourage the child to make a good decision to solve the problem. Verbalize your belief that the child has the ability to make positive decisions on his or her own behalf and to resolve the issue that led to the aggressive behavior.

- Make sure that you hold the child responsible for his or her behavioral decisions. In other words, *respond* to the child in ways that reinforce responsibility and consequences of choices rather than *react* in ways that mistakenly move the focus away from the child and onto yourself.

- If the child's behavior improves, no matter how minute the improvement, affirm the child's feelings and efforts to make positive decisions by communicating your understanding of how frustrated, angry, anxious, and so forth the child must be while congratulating him or her for any demonstrations of self-control.

- If the aggressive behavior continues, immediately intervene with a reasonable consequence. If the behavior escalates, do not wait to respond, thereby allowing the event to become a major incident that may be dangerous to you, the child, others, or the environment. Explain the reason behind your decision to intervene and stop a behavior. Children must understand the motivation for your intervention as protection and care, not anger.

Therapeutic Management of the Behavior of the Passive-Aggressive Personality

We must be self-aware in order to avoid being deceived by the passive-aggressive child. With self-awareness, we can choose to disengage from the passive-aggressive child emotionally and avoid reinforcing this type of behavior. Being self-aware also prevents us from being the victim of the child's predictable and destructive ways of engaging us in acting-out behavior.

In addition, we must acknowledge our normal feelings of anger toward the passive-aggressive child. Acknowledging our anger is an important skill because this child is unable to acknowledge feelings of anger. Unlike the passive-aggressive child, we can elect to acknowledge our anger while choosing not to express it in unhealthy ways, through our own aggressive or passive-aggressive behavior.

The passive-aggressive child can cause others to respond with counter passive-aggressive feelings and behaviors. Once we recognize and own these feelings and behaviors, as adults we must make a decision to refrain from all passive-aggressive behaviors in reaction to the child. We can stop this by ceasing all you-messages and replacing them with I-messages. This response demonstrates the ability to be honest about feelings and behaviors to the passive-aggressive child, who has learned to be dishonest and fearful regarding personal feelings and behaviors.

Passive-aggressive children must not be empowered by adults in situations where they can demonstrate passive-aggressive behaviors. Do not give this child control of the situation by making statements such as "We cannot move on with our activity until you take your feet off the table." Situations such as these empower the child and give him or her the opportunity to express anger inappropriately (i.e., passively).

When control of a situation is given to a passive-aggressive child, the comfort level of the other children in the setting can be dramatically decreased, and the adult and child can find themselves in a severe power struggle. Often in these situations, the adult loses control, which ultimately reinforces the child's belief that it is dangerous and inappropriate to express anger directly and openly.

Most passive-aggressive children are conscious of their behavior and the motivations behind their behaviors. These children's passive-aggressive behaviors must be benignly confronted. Benign confrontation is a verbal technique that requires the adult to make the child uncomfortable with his or her behavior without becoming so aggressive or confrontational that the child ceases communication or is reinforced in his or her beliefs about expressing anger. In benign confrontation, the adult openly shares thoughts about the child's behavior and the unexpressed anger behind the passive-aggressive behavior. The confrontation serves the purpose of communicating to the child that the adult is aware of the behavior and the purpose of the behavior. It also informs the child that the adult will not accept manipulative and controlling behavior as a way of expressing anger.

Therapeutic Management of the Behavior of the Withdrawn/Depressed Personality

Withdrawn/depressed children require assurance that they are not alone and that the helping adults in their world care about their lives and their circumstances. Constant affirmations and genuine listening can be effective strategies for keeping the depressed/withdrawn child engaged. Specific suggestions include the following:

- Make every attempt to initiate positive contact with the child immediately. The child must feel supported and that he or she has someone to speak with and confide in when feelings of intense sadness emerge.

- When the child is under stress, allow him or her to talk and express all feelings. Do *not* negate the child's depressed feelings; rather, help the child develop behavioral alternatives or strategies in response to these feelings.

- If the child is unable or unwilling to verbally communicate about the depressed feelings, encourage the child to use the written word to express them. Writing in personal journals is an effective strategy for the expression of thoughts and feelings.

- Encourage the child, particularly the younger child, to use pictures or other forms of creative expression, such as poetry and story writing, to communicate thoughts and feelings.

- Involve the child in the planning of future events. Offer special jobs or tasks the child is likely to enjoy. Having these opportunities can help the child shift thoughts and feelings from hopelessness (in extreme cases, possibly suicide) to involvement in these pleasant future events.

- Involve others who are a part of the child's team or who interact with the child so that the child will have a number of adults who are willing to discuss the depressed thoughts and feelings when the child needs immediate attention.

- Encourage the child to be open when he or she feels over-whelmed by depressed feelings and thoughts. Develop a way that the child can communicate with you—for example, a special signal or code—that alerts you that the child needs immediate attention.

- Assign the child a "buddy" who is able to assist the child in times of crisis and who has shown an interest in the child's well-being. When using this strategy, ensure that the buddy is able to handle the responsibility and not become over-whelmed.

In cases where the child expresses thoughts of suicide, it will be important to refer the child to a professional therapist or counselor for additional support.

Therapeutic Management of the Behavior of the Dependent Personality

The dependent child must be encouraged to participate in as many independent activities as possible. The following suggestions will help in achieving this goal:

- Do *not* allow the dependent child to become a constant companion to adults. This child should be encouraged to interact with peers in as many ways as possible.

- Allow the child to make simple independent decisions, such as about what games to play, what food to eat, or where he or she will sit, in order to give the child practice in decision making.

- Provide assurance that the dependent child is competent and can successfully take on tasks.
- Constantly offer abundant affirmations and genuine compliments.
- Assist the dependent child with accepting disappointment, sadness, and frustration. Because this child has learned to equate these feelings with rejection, he or she will need support in managing these feelings while maintaining a level of independence and control.
- Encourage overall independence, acceptance of responsibility, and competence. Because this child feels unable to be independent, responsible, or competent, any attempts in these areas must be encouraged and reinforced.

In conclusion, establishment of the healing environment enables us to care for and nurture children and youth in their daily surroundings. At this time in our society, the presence of the healing environment is critical. In this type of environment, supported by the efforts of caring and skilled adults, children can experience compassion, generosity, connectedness, trustful relationships, respect, and healing of their wounds. All of these elements are necessary for demonstration of positive behavior and development of the human spirit.

6

[An adult] needs a variety of intervention skills to maintain the on-going program. These "on the spot" skills are used for different reasons. One set of skills is targeted to prevent problem behaviors from developing by increasing desirable student behavior. [Another] set of skills is intended to decrease inappropriate student behavior by direct [adult] intervention.

—Nicholas J. Long and William C. Morse
(1996)

Tool 5: Surface Behavior Management Techniques

Not every behavior requires an in-depth response. There are times when we are required to respond to the "garden variety" behavioral challenges of children and youth as simply as possible. In these cases, Tool 5, Surface Behavior Management Techniques are effective, efficient, simple ways of addressing surface behavior. Figure 7 shows some of the benefits of using these techniques.

USING SURFACE BEHAVIOR MANAGEMENT TECHNIQUES

If there are behaviors that merely need to be managed, what are they, and how can we manage them? In general, SBMT's are best used in the following instances:

- When you determine that the behavior is not a symptom of an underlying issue *or* you determine that the behavior is a symptom of an underlying issue that cannot be addressed at that specific time
- When the behavior must be addressed immediately
- When you determine that the immediate goal is to manage the behavior
- When you determine that the behavior must be immediately stopped in order to protect the child, peers or adults, the environment, or the building or property
- When you determine that a specific SBMT is the simplest way possible to achieve the desired behavioral outcome

FIGURE 7
Benefits of Using SBMT's

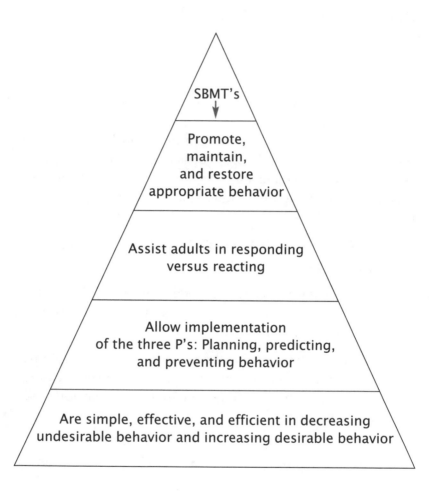

SBMT's

Promote, maintain, and restore appropriate behavior

Assist adults in responding versus reacting

Allow implementation of the three P's: Planning, predicting, and preventing behavior

Are simple, effective, and efficient in decreasing undesirable behavior and increasing desirable behavior

- When the child is in need of external methods to help him or her control misbehavior

In deciding whether to respond to a behavior with an SBMT or to employ a different type of response, we must remember to ask ourselves three questions: (a) What purpose does this behavior serve for this child; in other words, what need is this behavior meeting? (b) What am I hoping to accomplish in responding this way? and (c) What do I believe the child needs from me in order to make the best behavioral decisions?

CHOICES IN MANAGING SURFACE BEHAVIOR: PERMITTING, TOLERATING, STOPPING, AND PREVENTING

Tool 5 assists us in remembering that we have choices in managing the surface behavior of children and youth. Long and Newman (1996) tell us that there are four specific responses we can make when addressing behavior: permitting behavior, tolerating behavior, stopping behavior, and preventing behavior. When using SBMT's, we must be clear about why we have chosen a particular response to a particular behavior. Remembering these four alternatives in managing behavior will help us to identify the specific SBMT's to use and understand the reasons for our choices.

Permitting Behavior

Permitting behavior serves children because it communicates the message that we will allow the demonstration of specific desirable behaviors. If it is important for children to know what they cannot do, it is equally important for them to know what they can do. Children are reassured when they know in advance that a certain behavior will meet with an adult's approval rather than disapproval. Permitting certain behaviors also eliminates the need for children to constantly and unnecessarily test the limits of the adults in the setting and the limits of the setting itself. We must be clear with children regarding what behaviors we will accept and applaud. We may also permit a behavior that may be a little uncomfortable for us because we know that the natural consequences of the behavior will teach a more significant lesson than the consequences we may enforce.

Tolerating Behavior

Tolerating behavior serves children because it communicates our willingness to be flexible and accepting of them and their needs. While these behaviors may be tolerated under certain circumstances, this is not to say that they will be tolerated at all times. We may choose to tolerate behaviors that are less than ideal simply to get at a bigger issue—for instance, if the behaviors demonstrate successive approximations toward a desired behavioral goal. Or we may choose not to preoccupy ourselves and use our time with behaviors that are of lesser importance. We may also decide to tolerate certain behaviors under the following specific circumstances:

- If "learner's leeway" is appropriate. This means that adults will tolerate mistakes and certain behavioral responses when a child is learning a new skill and experimenting with new ideas.

- When children's behavior is reflective of a developmental stage. Adults may tolerate behavior that is typical and normal for a child of a particular age or in a particular developmental phase. (This is not to be confused with sanctioning behavior that is inappropriate for unrelated reasons.)

- When children's behavior is symptomatic of an underlying condition. It is appropriate for adults to tolerate behavior over which the child may have little or no direct control. In this case, we must realize that behaviors are often symptoms of emotional, psychological, and physiological issues and may be the only way the child is able to express his or her feelings.

Stopping Behavior

There are behaviors that we simply must stop in order to maintain order and safety, to allow learning to take place, and to maintain the basic values of the environment. Too often, however, we stop behaviors because of inconsistent limits and rules, when our own personal tolerance levels have been exceeded, or when we become overwhelmed with counteraggressive feelings toward children. Under these circumstances, we may respond to surface behaviors in ways that are too severe or inappropriate in other ways.

Children should be given very clear messages regarding behaviors that will be stopped. Before making a choice to stop a behavior, we must ask ourselves why we are intervening. It is also important to explain to children why we are stopping their behavior. By explaining, we use this opportunity to teach what is acceptable, what is not acceptable, and the reasons why. This explanation also minimizes children's tendency to invent their own explanations (e.g., "She doesn't like me" or "He doesn't want me to have fun" or "They want to embarrass me").

Preventing Behavior

Preventing behavior proactively addresses the surface behavior of children and youth. Adults can and should be able to predict and plan for situations in which acting-out behavior can be prevented. The options for preventing behavior include (a) reorganizing the classroom structure or events to minimize the opportunity for challenging behaviors, (b) removing a child from a volatile situation, and (c) structuring the environment in such a way that potential crisis situations are addressed prior to actual crisis events and the resulting problem behaviors. In these instances, preventing behavior is preferable to reacting and intervening after a crisis has taken place.

SUCCESSFUL IMPLEMENTATION OF SURFACE BEHAVIOR MANAGEMENT TECHNIQUES

We must be mindful of several factors if we are to use SBMT's effectively. These factors include the following:

- *Demonstration of genuine kindness and authentic caring.* The SBMT used is much more likely to be effective when children understand that you are using the techniques because you care for them rather than desire to control them.

- *Understanding of the developmental frame of reference.* Children are in need of different interventions based on their developmental stage. What works in addressing the behavior of a 6-year-old is very different from what works for a 14-year-old!

- *Development of genuine relationships with children.* Children who understand that you have a genuine relationship with them are much more likely to respond positively to your direction. The nature of your relationship can make the difference between a child's responding to your use of an SBMT or ignoring your use of an SBMT.

- *Understanding of the causes of behavior.* When you understand the causes of a behavior, you also understand what is necessary to address that behavior. There are a variety of reasons why children do what they do. When you have insight into these reasons, your choice of SBMT's will be more appropriate.

- *Development of structure and consistent adherence to it.* The decision to use SBMT's must be a part of an overall structure addressing the surface behavior of children. SBMT's are not a cure-all. They are a small portion of a larger picture in managing children's behavior.

- *Willingness to think outside of your own understanding and experience.* When we allow ourselves to remember that a child may be experiencing something outside of our understanding and life experience, we can use SBMT's with more compassion, empathy, and understanding.

- *Adoption of new patterns of personal behavior, if necessary.* SMBT's can support us in trying on new behaviors once we have exhausted our usual responses to a child's behavior.

Finally, we have dozens of SBMT's at our disposal when intervening in the behavior of youth. Several commonly used SBMT's are defined in Appendix D. When we have simple, effective, and efficient techniques available to us, we are much more likely to be successful in our attempts to manage behavior. It is important to keep in mind that our attempts to manage surface behavior serve the larger purpose of providing children with opportunities to practice how to learn, live, and interact with others.

7

*Talking creates conditions in which motivation
to change develops and builds students' trust in
adults sufficiently to accept guidance. The more
skilled we are in talking with students, the more
effective we will be in helping them learn to
manage their own problems. With
understanding and sensitivity to students'
feelings and the circumstances surrounding
incidents, we can provide the emotional support
they need while we teach them to solve problems
more effectively and with more satisfying
results.*

—Nicholas J. Long, Mary M. Wood,
and Frank A. Fecser (2001)

Tool 6: Effective Communication

Tool 6, Effective Communication, is the final tool of Positive Behavior Facilitation. Communicating with children and youth, particularly in times of conflict, involves many more skills than those we use in ordinary conversation. Our goal is to interact in ways that open communication rather than close communication. Our skills in this area can make a great difference for the children we serve and can determine whether they begin to believe that talking out is more functional than acting out their issues.

SIX SKILLS OF EFFECTIVE COMMUNICATION

When we communicate with children and youth in an effort to facilitate positive behavior, we use many skills. Effective communication involves the skills of observing, attending, listening, decoding, signaling, and responding (see Figure 8). These skills represent the six necessary elements of successful communication with children and youth.

Observing

Observing skills are necessary when we are looking for the hints or "nuggets" children are constantly dropping about the causes for their behavior. Many of these nuggets are nonverbal and require keen observation skills from adults. We must also closely observe children in order to take note of any nuances or differences in their behaviors on a particular day or in a particular circumstance. Our observation skills allow us to collect

FIGURE 8
Skills for Effective Communication

The skill of
RESPONDING

The skill of
OBSERVING

The skill of
SIGNALING

**EFFECTIVE
COMMUNICATION**

The skill of
ATTENDING

The skill of
DECODING

The skill of
LISTENING

important data about children and the emotional state in which we find them.

Attending

Attending skills allow us to pay specific attention to the needs of children, particularly in times of crisis or upset. When we are attending to children, we may offer them water, a tissue, or simply a place to sit. Attending communicates interest and care to the child, who is in need of our full attention and our best efforts.

Listening

Listening is a sophisticated skill and involves much more than being silent when someone else is speaking. In *The Lost Art of Listening,* Nicholas (1995) refers to this skill as "suspending our preoccupation with ourselves and entering into the experience of the other person . . . the stuff of human connection" (p. 10). We must learn to listen with our whole selves, including our ears, eyes, brains, and hearts. When we listen to children effectively, we are able to hear what is being said and what is not being said. Because nonverbal messages are much more authentic than verbal communications, we must become experts at listening to what children are telling us with their bodies, their tone of voice, and their facial expressions.

Decoding

Decoding involves our ability to make sense of behaviors and connect those behaviors directly to feelings. When we are challenged by children's behaviors, it is easy to believe that the behaviors are the critical factor. In truth, the behaviors are not the most critical factor in an incident; the feelings behind the behavior are the most critical. Decoding enables us to decipher what children are doing, move beyond the challenging surface behaviors of children, and make meaningful connections between their behaviors and feelings. This skill allows us to better understand children and their motivations. In addition, when children begin to learn to decode their own behavior, they are better able to understand themselves and the reasons they behave in certain ways.

Signaling

Signaling examines the skill of sending specific messages that are supportive and communicate our desire to assist children in resolving conflict and crises. Our signals to children are largely nonverbal, and many times we are unaware of the signals we are sending. Because children pay very close attention to us and are adept at reading our signals, it is critical that we be aware of and thoughtful about the signals we send.

Signaling involves the purposeful use of our bodies, eye contact, tone of voice, facial and hand gestures, and space and props in the environment. One of the misconceptions that we, as adults, hold is that our words are the most important part of any communication. In fact, our nonverbal communications speak much louder than any verbal messages we deliver. Have you ever heard the saying, "Do what I say, not what I do"? Ensuring that we are authentically communicating with children is crucial, particularly when we remember that children are constantly scrutinizing our signals for any discrepancies between what we say and what we do.

Responding

Responding with skill is necessary because our responses to children either increase or decrease the likelihood of crisis resolution. Many times our responses are, in fact, reactions. Reactions are based upon our emotions; however, responses are based upon our logical thoughts. Responding to children in ways that help them rather than harm them requires us to be thoughtful and clear about our intentions and what we desire the result of a particular situation to be. Our responses can determine if children are able to leave an incident with the belief that adults are willing and able to assist them or that adults are incapable and do not wish to assist them.

Mindful responses are a requirement for effective communication. Many adults say they want to help children, yet their responses communicate something different. When this happens, our ability to be supportive and form meaningful relationships with children is greatly impaired. When we learn to effectively and authentically respond with our whole selves, our ability to support children greatly increases.

THE IMPORTANCE OF EFFECTIVE COMMUNICATION

How do we know if or when we have been effective in our communications with children and youth? If we have been effective, their behaviors become less of a mystery and source of frustration for us. Through effective communication, we can begin to understand the needs of children and assist them in making choices that are self-supportive versus self-defeating. Effective communication is central to PBF because it is through communication that we begin to understand the circumstances and events of our children's lives. The skill of entering into a child's "life space" (Redl, 1959b) in ways that allow the child to be comfortable is primarily mastered through the knowledge and use of the tool of effective communication. When we reach a level of understanding of the challenges our children face, we are better able to be empathic to their struggles and offer support in ways that facilitate positive behavior.

Because communication is the foundation for all relationships, it is vital to our success in our work that we develop and practice being clear and supportive communicators. When our pathways of communication are not clear (i.e., when they are cluttered with our own "stuff"), we cannot listen, speak, and be heard in ways that are authentic and helpful to ourselves, to each other, or to children. The tool of effective communication reminds us that intervening in behavior requires us to be as authentic, clear, and cooperative as possible in our interactions with those around us, including children and adults.

DO'S AND DON'TS OF EFFECTIVE COMMUNICATION

When we are communicating with children and youth, it benefits us to understand those actions that can create opportunities for open and honest exchanges between adults and children and those that destroy those opportunities. The following do's can support us in talking with children in ways that help us to achieve the goal of mutual understanding and support.

Do . . .

- Try to get the child's point of view/frame of reference.
- Remember that a child in crisis has compromised communication skills.
- Have a "road map" that guides the direction of the conversation and is based on the child's presenting problem.
- Listen with an open mind.
- Model the behaviors you would like to see from the child.
- Express your genuine interest in helping the child, *but only if it's genuine.*
- Allow the child some time to vent his or her frustrations and to express the "flooded feelings."
- Make the child as comfortable as possible.
- Reinforce any attempts the child makes at conveying the problem verbally as opposed to behaviorally.

The following don'ts create barriers between adults and children and frustrate the goals of support and understanding.

Don't . . .

- Deliver a sermon; if you're talking more than the child, you're talking too much.
- Interrupt the child constantly.
- Judge what the child is saying; this is not your time to be "right."
- Deliver the consequences before understanding the issues and the behavioral offense(s).
- Bring in other adults and children to validate your point of view.

- Communicate with a child when you are emotionally upset and emotionally flooded yourself.

- End a communication with a focus on the problem; make sure you discuss the solution to the problem.

- Assign a time frame to a communication; if you have limited time, don't begin a communication that may be longer than the time you have available.

- Be uncomfortable with silence; silence can allow you and the child to become focused on what to say and how to say it.

- Begin a communication with a child while he or she is still emotionally charged and flooded.

- Use conversations with children as punishment (e.g., "If you don't behave, we will have to go and talk about it!").

SKILL-RELATED ABILITIES IN EFFECTIVE COMMUNICATION

As we take a further look at this topic, we learn that there are specific abilities related to each of the six skills of effective communication. The following descriptions present those abilities and pose questions related to the use of each skill.

Observing Abilities

The skill of observing involves the following abilities:

- Looking for what is not being said
- Careful and close examination of child behavior
- Discerning meaning from behavior
- Looking for the spoken—and unspoken—"nuggets" that children drop
- Watching for discrepancies and differences in usual behavior

When observing, ask yourself the following questions:

1. Am I watching carefully for nuances in the child's behavior?

2. Do I hear what is being said (verbally) and what is not being said (nonverbally) through behavior?

3. Do I recognize behaviors that indicate a child is under stress?

4. Am I able to observe a child without making him or her feel uncomfortable?

5. Are my observations based on what I am seeing or what I am feeling?

6. What behaviors have I observed that may need further exploration?

Attending Abilities

The skill of attending includes these abilities:

- Using physical space and objects to support communication
- Using nonverbal communications effectively
- Using one's voice and gestures to convey a message
- Accessing the appropriate energy level for the occasion
- Using time effectively and efficiently
- Being psychologically available to the child
- Appreciating the child's point of view

When attending, ask yourself the following questions:

1. Am I conveying interest and support?

2. Do my communications encourage dialogue and keep it going?

3. Am I providing help and support to the child in crisis?

4. Do my skills and the practice of these skills help create or destroy relationships?

5. What is my own body language communicating?

6. Do I have feelings or issues that get in the way of my ability to attend to this child?

7. Am I open to appreciating the child's point of view of the crisis situation?

8. Am I psychologically as well as physically present?

9. Am I able to take care of the child's needs so that the crisis situation can be examined and eventually resolved?

Listening Abilities

The skill of listening includes the following abilities:

- Using verbal and nonverbal messages
- Hearing, observing, and diagnosing nonverbal behavior
- Reading between the lines
- Listening with the whole self

When listening, ask yourself the following questions:

1. Am I listening in order to gather the information about the incident and the child's perspective of the incident?

2. Am I listening to what is being said and what is not being said, and can I diagnose/analyze what is not being said?

3. Am I listening for the "little nugget" that children always drop in order to give me insight into the crisis situation?

4. Can I place myself in the "psychological shoes" of the child while I am listening and once I have listened carefully?

5. Does my listening allow me to see the connection between the event, the child's feelings, and the child's behavior?

Decoding Abilities

The skill of decoding includes these abilities:

- Helping a child sort out any confused feelings
- Focusing on the child's perceptions of the events
- Asking clarifying questions (who, what, when, how, to what degree, etc.)
- Connecting behavior to feelings
- Understanding how feelings drive behavior
- Assisting a child in understanding what has happened

- Enabling a child to accept "flooded" feelings and find alternatives for acting-out behavior

When decoding, ask yourself the following questions:

1. Am I helping the child first to focus upon thoughts, second to focus upon feelings, and third to examine behavior in order that a connection can be made between all three (thoughts, feelings, and behavior)?

2. Do I understand how feelings drive behavior?

3. Am I assisting the child in seeing how his or her thoughts and feelings about a stressful event lead to specific behaviors?

4. Am I responding solely to the words that the child says?

5. Am I able to detect the meaning behind the words (decoding)?

6. Do I (a) decode the child's words to express feelings, (b) connect those feelings to their source, and (c) allow the child to talk about his or her feelings and stress?

Signaling Abilities

The skill of signaling includes the following abilities:

- Using both verbal and nonverbal messages
- Being self-aware about personal communication
- "Speaking" without talking
- Conveying messages authentically and honestly
- Using the whole self in communication

When signaling, ask yourself the following questions:

1. Am I communicating in such a way that my intentions are in alignment with the signals I am sending?

2. Am I communicating honestly, or am I trying to fool the child and/or myself about what I am feeling?

3. Are the signals I am sending helpful to the child at this time?

4. What are the signals I am sending, and am I in control of the messages my signals communicate?

5. Is care and concern reflected in my signals?

6. What signals am I sending that are supportive to the child, and what signals am I sending that may increase stress for the child?

Responding Abilities

The skill of responding includes the following abilities:

- Selecting a helpful response to the event
- Demonstrating empathy
- Offering abundant affirmations
- If appropriate, using nonthreatening confrontation
- Monitoring and controlling your feelings and behaviors
- Using clear communications in the midst of the child's confusing communications

When responding, ask yourself the following questions:

1. Am I listening carefully and examining all of the parts of the crisis before responding?

2. Am I affirming the child enough in order to communicate that we are on the same side, in an effort to resolve the situation?

3. Am I able to express empathy for the child and affirm the child for trying his or her best to resolve the crisis situation?

4. If I confront the child, have I done so in a way that is nonthreatening and nonaggressive?

5. Have I given my responses careful and logical thought before I speak?

6. Have I examined the purposes of my responses?

7. Do I discuss alternatives for the child's behavior and help him or her problem-solve around those alternatives?

8. Am I managing my own emotions, or am I reacting because of my own flooded feelings?

9. Are the questions that I am asking nonjudgmental and working in ways to gather information rather than to place blame?

10. Are my communications clear, or do they contribute to the child's confusion?

11. While responding, am I aware of the verbal and nonverbal messages I am sending?

THE LISTEN, RESPOND, TEACH (LRT) METHOD: EFFECTIVE COMMUNICATION WITH ADULTS

Effective communication also extends to our ability to communicate and collaborate with one another—adult to adult and colleague to colleague. Just as the communication skills of children and youth are compromised in times of conflict and crisis, we must remember that the communication skills of adults are also affected in times of mental or emotional upset. If we are able to focus on what the best possible outcomes are for the children and youth in our care, we can respond to the behavior and communications of adults, rather than react to them. The Listen, Respond, and Teach (LRT) method is designed to support adults in communicating clearly and effectively with other adults in the environment so that the children in the setting receive the highest quality of support and education possible.

One of the questions I am most frequently asked to answer is "What am I supposed to do about communicating with my co-workers? I don't have any problems communicating with kids; it's the adults who drive me crazy!" Because we know that children are always observing us and learning from us, the ways in which we communicate with the adults in our environment are just as critical as the ways in which we communicate with children. The LRT method supports us in remembering three simple steps when communicating with other adults— particularly in difficult or challenging circumstances. This method supports our being able to listen (L) to, respond (R) to, and teach (T) other adults.

When we can carry out the three steps of the LRT method, we are much more likely to have effective communications, even if we do not agree about events or circumstances. The goals of this method are similar to the goals we have when communicating with children: to keep pathways of communication open, to listen to and be heard by others, and to offer our support in resolving any issues. The steps of the LRT method are as follows.

Listen

- Be as nonjudgmental and open-minded as possible.
- Listen for the point of view of the adult.
- See the adult in a positive way, even when he or she does not behave positively.
- Remember that any behaviors or words are not to be taken personally!

Respond

- Always respond (logical thought) versus react (emotional expression).
- De-escalate yourself first and then de-escalate any acting-out behaviors of the adult.
- Offer your best efforts and do your best work with the adult.
- Believe that the adult wants to resolve conflict, just as you do.
- Remember that the adult in front of you has feelings.

Teach

- Teach only when the invitation has been extended to you.
- Remind yourself of your role as a supporter and educator of others.

- Offer options and alternatives for the adult to consider.
- Impart any information in a way that "speaks to" the adult (i.e., that takes into consideration where the adult is).
- Consider the operating frame of reference, beliefs, values, and background of the adult and teach with this information in mind.

If we are to move beyond sheer management of the behavior of children and youth, "respectful communications" (Brendtro & Shahbazian, 2004)—using all of the skills examined here—must be our goal. Supporting the behavioral change of another person requires that we enter into the life experience of the other person, which is the beginning of moving beyond management of behavior. Without the ability to communicate effectively with another person, our interactions will be polite and superficial at best. PBF calls on us to accept the challenge of joining with other human beings—children and adults alike—in an effort to understand them, hear them, support them, and provide a safe place for them to experience a heart-felt connection, as they determine how best to change their own lives.

Some seem to be born with a nearly completed puzzle.
And so it goes,
Souls going this way and that
trying to assemble the myriad parts.

But know this. No one has within themselves
All the pieces to their puzzle.
Like before the days when they used to seal
jigsaw puzzles in cellophane. Insuring that
all the pieces were there.

Everyone carries with them at least one and probably
Many pieces to someone else's puzzle.
Sometimes they know it.
Sometimes they don't.

And when you present your piece
Which is worthless to you,
To another, whether you know it or not,
Whether they know it or not,

You are a messenger from the Most High.

—Lawrence Kushner (2000)

Conclusion

You, as Messenger

At the beginning of this book, I shared with you that Positive Behavior Facilitation was born because of conversations I kept having about behavior management. Now that this particular project comes to an end, I realize that the broader conversation, for me, will never end. It may have been my belief that with enough thoughts, programs, philosophies, and dedicated people, somehow the discussion about how we best support our children would one day come to a close. On that day, I imagined, we would be doing what is best for children, as opposed to talking about what is best for children. However, today I know that the effort to move from conversation to action will not end. I realize that what I am up to, and what PBF is about, is a movement. This is the movement to change the way we meet the needs of our children and youth, and worthwhile movements never truly end.

Nurturing, raising, educating, and supporting today's children are what many people, myself included, now call a movement, perhaps similar to what Malcolm Gladwell (2000) calls a "social epidemic." Throughout history, people have found themselves in organized efforts called movements to address issues that call for a shift in the world's consciousness and in its actions. In an effort to understand exactly what I am involved in, I looked up the words *movement* and *epidemic* and found the following in Webster's. For *movement,* I found this: "A series of organized activities working toward an objective; an organized effort to promote or attain an end; the act or process of moving, change of place or position or posture." The definition of the word *epidemic* included this: "Affecting or tending to affect a disproportionately large number of individuals within a population, community, or region at the same time."

Feeling a little overwhelmed by the enormity of the words but a little relieved that at least now I have words to define what I am involved in, I find I have arrived at yet another challenge. I must accept that being a part of a movement means resigning myself to the fact that most people in the movement don't have the opportunity to experience the resolution of the movement's issues. This acceptance means embracing these words from a speech by Martin Luther King Jr., delivered March 3, 1968, in Atlanta's Ebenezer Baptist Church: "And I guess one of the great agonies of life is that we are constantly trying to finish that which is unfinishable. It's well that you are trying. You may not see it. The dream may not be fulfilled, but it's just good that you have a desire to bring it into reality. It's well that it's in thine heart." I understand that, although we live in a world where we are encouraged to get everything we can in the quickest, easiest, and most convenient way possible, it doesn't excuse me from the movement or make my involvement any less necessary.

There have been books written about the movement concerning children and youth with titles such as *The Resilience Revolution* (Brendtro & Larson, 2006) and *Reclaiming Our Prodigal Sons and Daughters* (Larson & Brendtro, 2000). These works remind us that the task we have dedicated our lives to is much bigger than buying the next program or finding the right method to "fix" our children. Today, growing our children in such a way that they are successful and fulfilled, and that they become adults contributing to society, requires long-term commitment. It requires a willingness to say and do what others will not, and the ability to be in a state of discontent with what currently exists; this is the stuff of which movements are made.

Being part of a movement also requires that the individuals who make up the movement be willing to commit to something bigger than themselves and that they live in a way that reflects a distinctive way of being in the world. Because PBF is a philosophy that you live, not a program that you do, it also asks that you embrace and live by something that I call "The Charge of

PBF," spelled out in Appendix E. It is not necessary that you make this charge your entire life, but being in a movement requires that you make something your entire life. It means that you find something that counts for you and that you live your life according to that something, even when it's not convenient, even when no one is watching, and even when you don't necessarily feel like living according to it, whatever that is for you.

I believe that those of us who are willing to live in this way are messengers. Every movement that has changed a condition or a state of being in the world has had its messengers. Dr. King, one of the world's most influential and prolific messengers, describes movements in this way:

> Human progress is neither automatic nor inevitable. Every step toward the goal of justice requires sacrifice, suffering, and struggle; the tireless exertions and passionate concern of dedicated individuals. This is no time for apathy or complacency. This is a time for vigorous and positive action. (cited in Phillips, 1999, p. 105)

The greatest and most significant movements in our world's history have had many charismatic and powerful messengers. Along with Dr. King, messengers such as Mohandas Gandhi, Harriet Tubman, Abraham Lincoln, Mother Theresa, Michael J. Fox, Oprah Winfrey, John F. Kennedy, Marva Collins, Eleanor Roosevelt, Bill Gates, Marian Wright Edelman, and Muhammad Ali have all gained a typically unattainable level of fame and notoriety; however, they are not the only messengers of the movements they've supported. More commonly, and certainly more abundantly, the messengers of movements are people like you, who are reading this book. The messengers of movements include people who will never be famous but will change the face of our society nonetheless.

In the following passage, Shore (1999) tells us that not only can we change the face of society, but as messengers, our lives will change as well:

> All of us have strengths we need to share. . . By itself, even a massive new wave of talent serving in ways that are better

and more effective may not be enough to save these kids but it is one indispensable ingredient without which they have no chance at all. You may wonder if it is guaranteed that committing yourself of the task will change our country and their lives. It is not, but it is guaranteed to change yours. (p. 6, 8–9)

PBF invites us to embrace that change. PBF also asks you, as a messenger, not only to be thoughtful about the solutions to the concerns of this movement, but always to be willing to ask yourself and others the tough questions. In her seminal writing *The Schools We Deserve,* Diane Ravitch (1985) ends by asking a series of challenging questions about educational reform rather than providing the standard and easy answers that so many of us seek and live by. As did Ravich, PBF asks you to consider some tough questions. The questions that PBF poses are these:

- What is your level of willingness to move beyond the typical ways of understanding and intervening in behavior?
- How willing are you to look beyond and underneath of the behavior of another human being in order to find their soul?
- Are you able to look in the mirror and be truthful about who you are and what your behavior looks like?
- Are you able to manage your own thoughts and feelings, or have you made someone or something else responsible for what you think and how you feel?
- What are your personal wounds, and are you managing them or are they managing you?
- Are you aware of what compromises your personal behavior and what you can do to change or manage these factors?
- Do you create conflict with others, or do you work to resolve conflict with others?
- In your interactions with children, are you mostly managing behavior, or are you a change agent for behavior?
- What is the nature of the environment you present to the children you serve?

- How can you maximize the healing potential of your surroundings for the children you serve?

- How do you therapeutically address the behavior of children, particularly those with personalities that challenge you?

- How would you explain the ways in which you manage the behavior of children?

- Do you manage surface behavior for the benefit of children or for the purpose of control?

- As a communicator, what skills do you use well and what skills can you improve?

- What is the nature of your communications with other adults in your environment?

- How do you use your communication skills in challenging situations with adults?

- As a messenger in this movement, how do your words, your actions, and your life speak to others?

If you are willing to linger in the asking of these questions, PBF will have an impact on your life as a messenger. Most people spend a lifetime seeking answers outside themselves to the questions they believe are worthy. In contrast, messengers spend a lifetime asking themselves the worthy questions, with the understanding that the internal process of asking is as important as finding the answers.

Someone in a workshop once asked me this question: "How can I expect a child's behavior to be different when the environment teaches her the exact opposite of the behavior I am trying to teach?" There I was again, faced with another powerful question that I wondered how to answer. In the moment that I stood there, the image of a large and beautiful ceramic planter popped into my head. In my mind, the planter represented the child, and the question I pondered was this: "If the planter is filled with soot and ashes and chemicals, all things that stunt growth and ultimately prevent a healthy life, what can I add to it so a living thing *will* thrive?" As a result of this image and the question that had come to me so suddenly, I soon began presenting this dilemma to the educators in my workshops:

> Imagine you have a large planter filled with ashes and poisonous chemicals, things that will surely kill anything you attempt to grow. The child you are working with is the planter, and the ashes and chemicals are all that your planter contains. How can we get rid of the poisonous elements and replace them with elements that nurture growth? The only thing we cannot do is turn over the planter and spill out the contents— because that will leave the planter completely empty, with nothing at all inside. What do we do?

After a lively discussion, I ask the participants to offer their answers to the question of how they, who care so deeply for children, would rid a child of damaging elements and replace them with that which nurtures. Ultimately the group comes to the answer that PBF supports: We slowly introduce the new elements into the planter, and as we add them, slowly but surely, the contents that we want to remove rise to the top and eventually spill over the sides, creating a space for everything that will heal and nourish what we wish to grow in the planter. Why is this important? Because this is what PBF offers: a gentle replacement of that which harms children in exchange for that which grows them. PBF is my offering into the consciousness of those of us who care for children and, as most things that are new must be, I hope its introduction has been a gentle, yet life-producing, one.

Today, my expectations are high for PBF and the significance of its contribution to this movement. As a messenger, it is my hope (and my intention) that PBF will challenge the traditional models of discipline and control used by many adults. The distinction between these models and PBF is summarized in "The 25 Principles of PBF" (Appendix F). I hope you will find statements there that stimulate your thinking about how we can facilitate positive behavior in ourselves and in others. I hope PBF calls into question any model that begins with the examination of the child rather than an examination of the adults interacting with that child. I hope that PBF reminds us that effective intervention in behavior requires more than finding the right "tricks" so kids will do what we want them to do. For those of us who are willing to allow it, I hope and trust that PBF will provide some insight into these complex issues. Finally, it is my prayer that PBF inspires you, as messenger, to join me and remain in the movement, fully committed and engaged in the work of planting and nurturing life: that which Lorraine Monroe (1995) calls the worthiest work—the work of transforming children's lives.

The Language of PBF

Attitude

A state of mind in relation to some matter or situation; a mental or emotional position. _Commentary:_ The attitude of the mind toward a particular thing or condition determines the nature of and one's experience with that thing or condition. The attitude we have toward our work with children will directly affect the nature of our work and the experiences we have with children and our work.

Awareness

A knowledge or realization; a cognizant thought that allows for observation and/or action. _Commentary:_ Our level of awareness of ourselves is critical in our work with children. Once we are aware of something, we are then responsible for taking appropriate action regarding our awareness.

Behavior

An observable action resulting from one's thoughts and feelings; often a needs-based response or reaction to a particular circumstance, occurrence, or experience. _Commentary:_ All behavior has purpose and is the result of something (i.e., nothing comes from nothing). The behavior we see from children is the result of their thoughts and feelings regarding an experience or event of which we may or may not have knowledge.

Belief

An acceptance of an idea or concept as true; a precept that can function consciously or unconsciously. *Commentary:* Our beliefs are often instilled in us by others (parents, spouses, teachers, family members, society, etc.). Although we have not tested these beliefs to determine their truthfulness, we behave as if our beliefs are absolute facts. Our belief system dictates what we believe to be true about ourselves, our world, and others and will directly affect how we interact with ourselves and others.

Change

To be or make different; to transform; to be altered or modified, which involves the removal of one thing and the replacement of another. *Commentary:* The need or desire for change does not necessarily indicate that something is wrong with a current way of being. It indicates the desire or necessity for something to be different from its current state. We cannot change others; we can only change ourselves. We can support others in making the decision to change themselves by developing supportive relationships, creating healing environments, and offering suggestions that facilitate the desired change.

Comprehensive

Covering much; extensive; inclusive of a large scope; a broad range; limitless. *Commentary:* In order to address the behavior of today's youth, a comprehensive analysis of what behavior is, as well as why behavior takes place, is necessary.

Consciousness

A sense of awareness and knowing; internal awareness and perception; the knowledge of realization of an idea, object, or condition; the collective of all ideas, thoughts, emotions, and knowledge. *Commentary:* The level of one's consciousness and the recognition of one's own intentions, needs, feelings, and behaviors is directly related to the ability to grow and change.

Environment

Surroundings; milieu; external factors surrounding and affecting an organism at any time; forces that shape the life of a person. *Commentary:* The environment in which a human being exists generally plays a critical role in his or her thoughts, feelings, and behaviors.

Experience

Something personally lived through or encountered; the observing, encountering, and undergoing of things / occurrences; an event that takes place outside of but can be directly controlled by an individual; an event that can affect the individual. *Commentary:* As adults, we can create experiences for children that reinforce positive behavior and minimize negative behavior. An experience a child has with other children and adults in his or her environment can determine the quality of future experiences for that child.

Facilitate

To assist in the progress of; to make easier or less difficult; to help move forward. *Commentary:* As adults, although we cannot ultimately control the outcomes for children, a part of our role with children in our care is to facilitate their positive development, their independent thinking, and their successful living.

Heal

To restore to a state of perfection; to return to an original state of being; to make sound or whole; to repair or reconcile; to effect a cure. *Commentary:* Although we cannot heal another, we can heal ourselves. This personal state of wholeness is necessary for us if we seek to support another human being in doing the same.

Intention

A clear idea of desire; an act of determining mentally upon some action or result; purpose; purpose or attitude that affects one's actions or conduct. *Commentary:* Our intentions toward children and their well-being directly affect our behaviors and their resulting outcomes. If we consciously intend to support children in their growth and learning, we are more likely to create environments and have relationships with children that will help us realize this outcome.

Intervention

The act of interceding; mediating between; an interference in a state of affairs; the behavior of occurrence between events or people. *Commentary:* The quality of our interventions with children can either support positive behavior or undermine its demonstration/existence.

Management

The act or process of bringing about or succeeding in accomplishing; contriving; the act of handling or influencing; controlling in acting or use. *Commentary:* A part of our responsibility with children is the management of surface behavior that may interfere in their learning or development. We are in need of many management skills and techniques in order to support our children in the demonstration of positive behavior.

Needs

Perceived requirements; wants or desires; of necessity. *Commentary:* The needs of human beings dictate their behaviors. Our behaviors generally serve the purpose of having our needs satisfactorily met. We are often unconscious of the needs we are attempting to get met through our behaviors.

Nonjudgment

Not viewing or deciding about on the basis of the personal standards or opinions of others; not to make evaluation through comparison or contrast. *Commentary:* In order to operate in our children's best interest, we must begin from a place of nonjudgment as relates to who they are, what their circumstances are, and what behaviors they are demonstrating.

Relationship

A connection, association, or involvement; an emotional connection between persons. *Commentary:* The quality of the relationships we have with children can make a significant difference in their decisions about their lives, themselves, and the behaviors they will choose to demonstrate.

Resolution

The act of resolving or determining a course of action; firmness of purpose; the act of resolving; a solution or settlement of a problem; a resolve or determination. *Commentary:* A part of our task with children, particularly in times of crisis, is to support them in identifying resolutions to crisis events or events that create conflict for them. When moving toward resolution, children begin to take responsibility for their role in situations of conflict, learn to make better behavioral decisions for themselves, and identify behavioral alternatives in the event of similar occurrences.

Responsibility

Answerable or accountable for something within one's own power; willingness to accept consequences/effects related to one's self as the source, occasion, or cause for outcomes. *Commentary:* Adults serve as role models for children as they attempt to learn personal responsibility. Accepting full responsibility for one's thoughts, feelings, and behaviors is necessary for successful adult living.

Serve

To act as a servant; to render assistance; to be of use; to help; to have definite use; to contribute to. *Commentary:*

Our choice to serve children must be at the forefront of our decisions and our actions as we interact with those we serve.

Skill

The ability to do something well, arising from talent, training, or practice; special competence in performance; expertise. *Commentary:* We must consciously practice the skills that accompany the tools necessary to effectively serve the children in our care.

Strategy

A careful plan or method; a broad plan or method for achieving a goal; the devising or employing of plans toward a goal. *Commentary:* As supportive adults, we must employ strategies with input from children that will assist us in helping them successfully meet their goals.

Support

To bear or hold up; to provide for; to sustain; to uphold or advocate for; something that serves as a foundation; assistance. *Commentary:* Many of our children are living without the support of a caring adult. As these adults, we can offer support to children that can make the difference in their success or failure in realizing their life objectives.

Technique

The manner and ability with which someone uses the technical skills of a particular field; the body of specialized procedures and methods used in a specific field; a specific method used to accomplish something. *Commentary:* There are specific techniques available to adults who desire to support the children in their care. Adults must learn and master the techniques appropriate to encourage the demonstration of positive behaviors from children.

Tool

Anything used as a means of accomplishing a task or purpose; something used in performing an operation or something necessary in the practice of a profession. *Commentary:* Having the tools necessary to understand and intervene in the behavior of youth is one of the first steps in supporting the intellectual and social-emotional growth of children.

Strategies and Techniques for Behavior Management and Behavior Change

We can employ numerous techniques in order to manage the behavior of others or to support change in their behavior. Those listed below are examples of typical strategies that adults use to regulate and support behavior change in children and youth.

Surface Behavior Management Techniques (SBMT's)

SBMT's are simple and effective techniques used to promote, maintain, and/or restore appropriate behavior in the environment. These techniques are to be used when there is a need to respond to the surface behavior of children in ways that are simple, quick, and effective. Use of these techniques can decrease undesirable behavior and increase desirable behavior.

Rewards and consequences

The use of rewards and consequences relies on external control methods that assume the chosen consequence will stop misbehavior, while the chosen reward will serve as a motivator for desirable behavior. A system of rewards and consequences usually produces short-term results and allows a superficial management of behavior that may be necessary in emergencies and potentially volatile situations.

125

Discipline systems/rules

Systems of discipline are intended to prevent, suppress, and redirect misbehavior. The goal of discipline systems is to enforce rules in such a way that the need for adult intervention is reduced, thereby helping children learn to control their own behavior. In order to instill discipline in children, rules and standards must be enforced in such a way as to build cooperation and self-control so that disruptions are minimized and learning is maximized.

Code of conduct

A code of conduct specifies how everyone in an environment is to behave and interact. Ideally, a code of conduct is established jointly by adults and children; under the code, both adults and children are held accountable for their behavior at all times. Codes of conduct can replace a set of rules if they define the operating principles of the environment. Codes of conduct also include a set of consequences to be enforced when the code is violated.

Class meeting

Meetings at the classroom level reinforce the skills of accepting others, communicating effectively, showing respect, and maintaining a positive attitude. The purpose of class meetings is to assist children in seeing adults as partners and to reinforce a climate of mutual respect between the adults and youth. In effective class meetings, adults and children listen to one another, take one another seriously, and work together to solve problems for the benefit of all involved. Nelsen, Lott, and Glenn (2000) identify eight building blocks for effective class meetings. They are (a) form a circle, (b) practice compliments and appreciation, (c) create an agenda, (d) develop communication skills, (e) learn about separate realities, (f) recognize the four reasons people do what they do, (g) practice role-playing and brainstorming, and (h) focus on nonpunitive solutions.

Contracting

Contracting is a process for establishing written or verbal agreements between the adult and the child to provide a specific service, reward, or event in return for a specific behavior. The contract specifies the behavior that is being addressed and establishes deadlines for completion. Contracting involves reinforcement of desirable behavior, includes mutual goal setting between the adult and child, and teaches the skill of negotiation. The process for contracting includes four steps: (a) scheduling of the child/adult conference; (b) discussion with the child regarding the need for the contract; (c) establishment of the contract, including the specific terms (i.e., behaviors) to be targeted, people involved, and time frames, criteria for success, responsibilities of adult and child, and consequences of behavior; and (d) follow-up review and revision of contract, if necessary. The agreements are signed by any adults involved in the contract with the child.

Conferencing

Conferencing involves a private conversation with a child who is demonstrating unacceptable behavior. This can be a useful strategy because (a) it allows for an exchange of views in a confidential manner and setting, where the adult and the child can gain awareness of each other's views and feelings about the situation; and (b) it assists the child in understanding that the adult is concerned about him or her, even though the standards and expectations of the environment must be upheld. Conferencing will likely have to take place more than once in order to see a change in behavior from the child. In using conferencing as a strategy to address behavior, the adult must be careful not to sermonize (i.e., spend an extended time telling the child what he or she is doing wrong and must do in order to be right). The adult must also watch the child carefully to ensure that conferencing is not reinforcing the child's undesirable behavior, as some children will be reinforced by the conference and will perpetuate the undesirable behavior in order to gain attention from the adult.

Token economy

A token economy is a behavior modification system that involves accumulation of tangible reinforcers that can be saved and spent for privileges or items. As children comply with the behavioral guidelines and expectations of the environment, they accumulate tally marks, stamps on a card, tokens, or other tangible items that represent a "price" to be contributed toward a "purchase." In order for token economies to be effective, the adults must dispense the reinforcers quickly, easily, and consistently. The effectiveness of these systems also depends on the level of motivation the tokens and the eventual reinforcer provides for the child. Adults must ensure that children do not become too focused on the rewards, learn to ignore personal responsibility, or begin to expect that they will always receive tangible rewards for expected behaviors.

Level system

A level system uses a continuum of levels, each of which represents varying levels of privilege for children. Level systems generally use points that are collected in order to earn placement on a particular level. Movement between levels is based upon the accumulation of a specific number of points. On the basis of the level they have earned, children are able to engage in the privileges and activities that have been designated for that specific level. Level systems may use various ranking identifiers or descriptors, such as level 1, level 2, level 3, level 4; platinum level, gold level, silver level, copper level; or red level, yellow level, orange level, blue level. Adults who use level systems must ensure that record keeping regarding point accumulation is well organized, well monitored, and consistent. As children become more comfortable with the system, record keeping should be completed by the individual child and can be an activity used to teach personal responsibility. Because level systems represent a behavior management technique that is external to children, these systems should be used in conjunction with other strategies and techniques that promote internal behavioral change.

Point system

A point system uses the accumulation of numeric points that can be exchanged for privileges, activities, or rewards. Children are able to earn and lose points on the basis of demonstrated behaviors. Generally, points are recorded on point sheets, which identify specific behaviors, and are totaled at the end of the day to be calculated into a total number of points earned in a particular level (see level system, above.) In order for point systems to be effective, children and adults must keep accurate records regarding the points earned, the reinforcers being offered must be meaningful to the children, and reinforcers must be available on a consistent and fair basis.

Therapeutic Crisis Intervention (TCI)

TCI is a crisis prevention and intervention model. TCI assists professionals and organizations or programs in preventing crises from occurring, de-escalating crises, managing physical acting-out behavior, reducing potential injury to youth and staff, and teaching youth positive coping skills. TCI is oriented toward offering staff the tools necessary to support children and youth in learning developmentally appropriate and constructive ways of managing their feelings and their resulting behaviors. The primary goals of TCI are to (a) reduce or eliminate the need for physical interventions with children and youth; (b) provide professionals with the skills and knowledge necessary for them to become catalysts through which children can change destructive behavior patterns; (c) assist professionals in supporting children to develop self-supportive responses to their environments and circumstances; and (d) support children in achieving higher levels of social and emotional maturity.

Life Space Crisis Intervention (LSCI)

LSCI is a therapeutic and reality-based technique that provides helping adults with specific competencies to effectively intervene with children and youth in crisis. LSCI capitalizes on crisis events as opportunities for children to grow and teaches helping adults to maximize the opportunity for children to learn self-control and self-monitoring in times of crisis. LSCI provides instruction for helping adults to learn common self-defeating behavioral patterns of youth in crisis and offers specific strategies for examining and addressing these patterns. LSCI teaches helping adults three critical foundational skills for effectively addressing any challenging behavior. These skills are (a) understanding the differences in the worlds of children and helping adults, (b) understanding the dynamics of conflict and its cyclical pattern, and (c) understanding effective communication with children in crisis. LSCI offers helping adults a cognitive road map for helping children learn problem-solving techniques, self-supporting behaviors, and the personal insight necessary for behavioral change.

Interview

Interviewing children can serve many purposes that have a positive impact on a child's behavior. Interviewing can assist adults in building positive relationships with the children in their care. Children are much more susceptible to the influence of adults with whom they have a positive relationship. Generally, interviewing is conducted in one-on-one sessions in private settings. Each setting must be conducive to the child's comfort in order for the adult to learn as much as possible about the child. Interviewing assists adults in gaining information about a child's life circumstances. This information is very important in understanding the behavior of a child. Interviews can be conducted around specific behavioral events or, in general, in order to continue building relationships between the child and the adult.

Therapeutic milieu

Therapeutic milieu, a term coined by Fritz Redl (1959a), refers to the establishment and purposeful creation of an environment that is healthy and nurturing for the children in it. The therapeutic milieu includes specific facets, both tangible and intangible, that affect the performance and sense of well-being that children experience. Environments can have restorative or wounding powers for children. Therapeutic milieu capitalizes on the possibility of restoration of all children: The concept assumes that the setting in which a child functions has a direct relationship to the child's ability to learn and develop.

Therapeutic grouping

A therapeutic grouping is an arrangement of children or youth in a particular environment established to support members and maximize the group's positive attributes. Therapeutic groups consider a child's personality type, ability level, likes and dislikes, social relationships, chronological and developmental age, and strengths and deficiencies. Group dynamics are carefully observed and considered in placing a child within a specific group. When children are grouped therapeutically, specific attention is paid to children who may not do well together in group situations. When possible, these groupings are avoided, and every effort is made to create groupings that allow for positive interactions and maximal performance from all members.

Appendix C

Questions for Assessing the Healing Environment

Practice 1: Children as Thinkers

- Are children in the setting encouraged to think for themselves, or are they most frequently asked to comply with adult requests and directions?

- Do children have opportunities to make meaningful decisions about themselves and the occurrences in the setting?

- Do the lessons being taught include the development of critical thinking skills, or do the tasks consist largely of those that reinforce rote memorization and learning?

Practice 2: Behavior as a Teaching Tool

- Is the challenging behavior of children seen as an opportunity for children to grow, or is it viewed as problematic (i.e., something to be avoided and/or eliminated)?

- Do the adults in the setting understand the nature and causes of behavior so that they are able to respond rather than react to challenging behaviors?

- Does the setting use and adhere to an organized and logical sequence of consequences for child behavior that recognizes that consequences can be both positive and negative?

- How are consequences delivered to children and youth?

- Are children receiving consequences rather than being punished for their behaviors?

Practice 3: The Whole Being

- Does the setting acknowledge the importance of developing and teaching to children's emotional and internal state of being as well as their intellectual and external state of being?
- How are the emotional and behavioral needs of children addressed in the setting?
- Are the adults in the setting trained and prepared to address the emotional concerns of the children in the setting?

Practice 4: Teaching about the Self

- Do the adults have an understanding of their own behaviors and the motivations for their behaviors?
- How are the children in the setting encouraged to develop an understanding and appreciation of themselves?
- Do the adults in the setting understand the causes for behavior and reasons that children behave in certain ways so that they may offer insight to the children regarding their behaviors?

Practice 5: Why We Are Here

- Are the adults clear about their role in the setting and their primary function as related to meeting the needs of the children?
- How are the needs of the children in the setting met on a daily basis and by whom?
- Does the setting operate from a common philosophy, mission, and set of operating principles that guide the day-to-day practice of the adults in the environment?

Practice 6: Everyone and Everything Matters

- Does the setting recognize the importance of all that happens to and with children in the setting?
- Are all adults in the setting recognized with equal significance as relating to children's relationships and interactions?

- How are all adults and disciplines acknowledged and celebrated in the environment?

Practice 7: The Three R's: Respect Received Reciprocally

- Is respect understood as a function of positive relationships between children and adults rather than simply as what children do and don't do with adults?
- Do the adults freely and consistently respect the children in the setting on the basis of *who* the children are versus what their *behaviors* are?
- How are the behaviors of the adults reflective of respect for the children in the setting?

Practice 8: Relationships Are Everything

- What is the nature of the relationships between adults in the setting?
- What is the nature of the relationships between children in the setting?
- What is the nature of the relationships between adults and children in the setting?
- If relationships are in need of restoration, how is this done in the setting?

Practice 9: Happy Adults, Happy Children

- Are the adults celebrated in the setting?
- How do the adults celebrate in the setting?
- Do the adults in the setting feel appreciated and acknowledged?
- How are adults in the environment encouraged to be at their best with children?

Practice 10: Every Child Can

- Do the adults in the setting believe in the ability of all children—in other words, are the expectations high for all children?

- Are there children in the setting who consistently under-achieve, and if so, how are they supported so they are able to increase their level of performance?
- Are the children in the environment treated with consistency, fairness, and equality, or do some of the adults have certain "favorites" among the children who are treated differently or better than other children?

Appendix D

Definitions of Surface Behavior Management Techniques

Planned ignoring

Many children engage in negative behavior to receive attention from adults. The decision by adults to ignore or tolerate undesirable behavior so that it will decrease or extinguish itself is labeled planned ignoring. Part of the planfulness also includes paying positive attention to children's desirable behavior. Planned ignoring should not be used when children's negative behavior is potentially dangerous to the physical or psychological well-being of themselves, other children, or adults.

Stating expectations

Behavioral expectations must be clearly established, preferably with input and agreement from children. All adults are responsible for maintaining these rules in addition to any other standards or limits that will be emphasized in specific environments or situations. It is best to keep stated expectations to a minimum and to word them positively. All standards for behavior should be posted in every space that the children will occupy.

Support from restructuring

Disruptive behaviors can be regulated by restructuring or modifying the situation to bolster behavior control and decrease stress for the child. Modifications are possible in areas such as seating; grouping; degree of adult assistance; nature, format, and complexity of the task; physical movement; degree of involvement; amount of recognition; extent of decision making; and recognition and acceptance of personal feelings.

Signal interference

Many nonverbal cues can be used to curb negative behavior, thereby avoiding the need to name children or specifically verbalize the disruptive behavior. In some instances, children will benefit from signaling by saving face with their peers. The three major types of signaling are (a) facial expressions, such as eye contact; (b) body movement, such as clearing the throat or motioning with the head or hands; and (c) mechanical devices, such as repetitively turning lights off and on. Proximity control is a specific form of adult signal interference that consists of doing one or more of the following: (a) orienting one's body toward a child; (b) walking toward a child; (c) placing one hand on a child's desk, shoulder, or arm; and (d) touching or removing the object used by a child to create distraction. When using proximity control, adults must be fully aware of what they are doing at all times and should be able to identify those children who can tolerate being touched and those who cannot. Adults must also be cautious that the proximity is not misinterpreted by the child as threatening, sexual, intimidating, and the like.

Interest boosting

Many disruptive behaviors can be diverted or extinguished by appealing to children's interests. Interest boosting requires adults to know what a child's interests are and to insert these areas of interest in times of potential crisis. If adults use these interests, the child's attention can be diverted or refocused to the topic of interest and to circumstances that are less stressful for the child.

Antiseptic bouncing

Innocuous removal from a potential crisis situation allows the child to save face when redirected by adult instruction. Antiseptic bouncing allows adults to create situations in which the disruptive behavior can be minimized or avoided by removing the child or giving the child directions that cause him or her to be distracted from the situation. Asking a child to take a message to another adult, giving a child a task to complete outside of the classroom or in another area, and asking the child to change his or her location for reasons other than the child's own behavior are examples of antiseptic bouncing.

Warning

Consequences for undesirable behavior should be established in advance of any enforcement. All children must have a definite understanding that their negative behaviors can cause undesirable consequences. A warning is a reminder or restatement that a choice of continued unacceptable behavior will cause a negative outcome. When adults give this warning, the children have a clear and responsible choice to make. If multiple warnings are given, adults can be inadvertently sending the message that consequences will not be enforced or that adults are unwilling to issue consequences. If more than one warning is offered, children must be clear about how many warnings will be issued prior to actual consequence enforcement. If children continue to misbehave after warnings, it is assumed that they are either testing the limits and abilities of the adults to follow through or are prepared to accept the consequence that already has been given.

Support through humor

A humorous comment is able to penetrate a tense and possibly anxiety-producing situation. Support through humor clears the air and makes the child feel more comfortable. Therapeutic humor is a two-way experience in which both parties enjoy the situation. Adults must be mindful to avoid sarcasm, which is one-way humor, and put-downs, which humiliate children and are a form of social interaction in which one person finds pleasure while the other person experiences psychological pain. If humor is used, adults must be aware of the child's ability to understand the joke; in other words, adults must make sure that the humor is not misinterpreted by the child as a criticism or deprecating comment.

Support from routine

Using routine to reduce negative behaviors requires adults to structure and order situations and conditions that produce positive behaviors. Children are able to rely on an everyday routine, which minimizes stress and the possibility of crisis situations while increasing comfort levels and an understanding of the boundaries for behavior. Children should experience a regulated schedule that informs the expected activities throughout the day. While providing behavioral support through the use of routine, adults should also aid children in the understanding that, at times, deviations may occur because of specific circumstances or situations. Children should be able to return to the established routine as soon as possible.

Descriptive praise

The use of praise is a positive way of building up, or promoting, self-esteem and confidence. Positive reinforcers such as praise can accelerate a behavior, while negative reinforcers can decelerate the behavior. Descriptive praise amounts to much more than using the words great, terrific, and wonderful to describe a child. These general comments often have the opposite effect that the adult desires: Children may question the validity or sincerity of comments that are general in nature. Such comments may introduce additional pressure and cause feelings of inadequacy and guilt.

Descriptive praise tells children about their accomplishments, not their personalities. It deals with the children's efforts and behaviors without labeling them as "good" or "the best." Descriptive praise is also specific to a task or behavior (e.g., "Gerald, I noticed that you worked at your desk today for 15 minutes and when you were finished, you raised your hand. Thank you for demonstrating excellent study skills today"). The difference between general and descriptive praise allows the child to self-deliver messages about himself or herself after evaluating the adult's message. When children tell themselves that they are competent, the positive comments offered in descriptive praise promote self-esteem and investment in learning and positive behavior.

Direct appeal to values

Disruptive behaviors can be minimized or alleviated when adults assist children in realizing that their behavior violates the basic values of the environment, the group, or the individual. In doing so, adults must be conscious of their own values and whether the value being appealed to is shared by the children. When values and boundaries are clearly established, the appeal can be made to children based upon these expectations and limits in times of potential crisis. For example, if a program value is "We will not take things that do not belong to us" and if a child is tempted to demonstrate or demonstrates this behavior, the behavior can be alleviated by reminding the child (or all children) that the program value is that we do not steal, so the behavior of stealing is not acceptable within the boundaries of the setting. In this way, adults avoid the potential conflict that arises when children are expected to own the same values that adults do.

Physical restraint

In instances when a child completely loses control and is a threat to self or others (or is committing major property damage), physical restraint may be necessary. This technique is warranted only after all other measures of behavior management have been exhausted and only if it is used as a measure to protect, and not punish, a child. Adults must be specially trained to perform safe physical restraint and must be able to exercise control over their own feelings before attempting to apply these techniques. Children should not be expected to discuss and analyze the crisis situation during the restraint. After a restraint, the child and adults involved should discuss reasons for the restraint and any feelings the child may have regarding the restraint. This serves to strengthen trust.

Conferencing

Behaviors can be managed by arranging for a private or semiprivate conference between the child and an adult during which behavioral expectations are identified and communicated. This opportunity allows the child to gain awareness of expectations regarding behavioral performance. Conferencing provides the adult with an effective method of explaining the behavioral standards and limits of the environment and the consequences for infractions of these limits. While conferencing is considered to be an explanation of standards related to a particular behavior, adults should avoid sermonizing to children in an effort to decrease undesirable classroom behavior.

Enforcement of consequences

The enforcement of announced and agreed-upon consequences is critical to effective behavior management. Adults are accountable for preserving basic behavioral values and standards within the environment and should feel comfortable enforcing consequences when infractions occur, and enforcing consequences for behavior will decrease or extinguish undesirable behavior. When enforcing consequences, adults must be (a) immediate, (b) nonpunitive, and (c) consistent. When a decision has been made to enforce consequences, adults must examine their reasons using this strategy. If an adult is using consequences to punish or get back at a child, an adversarial relationship may result between the adult and child and between the adult and other children if these children observe the inappropriate implementation of the consequences. When the enforcement of consequences does not improve behavioral performance, new strategies must be identified and used. The continual enforcement of ineffective consequences serves only to reinforce undesirable behavior.

Appendix E

The Charge of PBF

1. I will remember that the behavior of others, including children and adults, is mostly about them and not about me.
2. I will consistently and honestly engage in self-examination and self-management.
3. I will acknowledge and respect the goodness that exists in everyone.
4. I will do my finest work with children to the best of my ability and at all times.
5. I will create environments for youth that are supportive, nurturing, and healing.
6. I will create and maintain clear pathways of communication with others by removing any clutter interfering with creating positive results.
7. I will manage the challenging behaviors of children with care, consistency, and commitment.
8. I will encourage and contribute to the positive behavioral change of others.
9. I will consciously work toward resolving conflict and will avoid creating conflict for myself and others.
10. I will accept personal responsibility for all of my thoughts, feelings, and behaviors and the results they create.

The 25 Principles of PBF

Principle 1

Behavior is not microwaveable. (In other words, changing it takes time.)

Principle 2

A tool is something used to get a job done. A skill is the result of consistent practice with tools.

Principle 3

You cannot change the behavior of another human being. You can form relationships and create environments that support others while they change themselves.

Principle 4

Relationships are the foundation for everything.

Principle 5

Being self-aware is the first step in living successfully. Managing what you become aware of is the second step.

Principle 6

Conflict and crisis are not the same thing.

Principle 7

Conflict is an opportunity for learning about yourself and others.

Principle 8

The healing environment is more about the nature of the relationships in the setting and less about what is in the physical setting.

Principle 9

Everyone is equally important to a child's growth and healing.

Principle 10

You have control over your thoughts, feelings, and actions.

Principle 11

Relief from conflict is not the same as resolution of conflict.

Principle 12

Someone or something else cannot trigger you.

Principle 13

Nonverbal messages are more authentic than verbal messages.

Principle 14

Adults and children have very similar needs.

Principle 15

Observable behavior is the most visible and least significant part of a human being.

Principle 16

The overuse of SBMT's can be addictive for adults and children.

Principle 17

Things manage behavior; people change behavior.

Principle 18

Your core beliefs will shape how you think, feel, and behave; know what they are. If the beliefs you now have no longer work for you, work to replace them with beliefs that do work for you.

Principle 19

There are many children and adults whose lives predispose them for conflict. In other words, their crisis often has nothing to do with you; you just happen to be present.

Principle 20

Supporting others in changing their behavior requires that you be in a relationship with them and that you get involved in their lives.

Principle 21

Before you attempt to manage and control the behavior of another, manage and control your own behavior.

Principle 22

All of your efforts will be more successful if you genuinely care about what you are doing.

Principle 23

Don't take it personally, even when it feels personal.

Principle 24

Learn to be comfortable with silence; it's a powerful tool.

Principle 25

You can't effectively intervene in what you don't understand.

References

Ayers, W. (1995). *To become a teacher: Making a difference in children's lives.* New York: Teachers College Press.

Benson, P.L. (1997). *All kids are our kids: What communities must do to raise caring and responsible children and adolescents.* San Francisco: Jossey-Bass.

Brendtro, L.K., Brokenleg, M., & Van Bockern, S. (1990). *Reclaiming youth at risk.* Bloomington, IN: National Education Service.

Brendtro, L.K., & du Toit, L. (2005). *Response ability pathways: Restoring bonds of respect.* Cape Town, South Africa: Pretext.

Brendtro, L.K., & Larson, S.J. (2006). *The resilience revolution.* Bloomington, IN: Solution Tree.

Brendtro, L.K., Ness, A., & Mitchell, M. (2001). *No disposable kids.* Longmont, CO: Sopris West.

Brendtro, L.K., & Shahbazian, M. (2004). *Troubled children and youth: Turning problems into opportunities.* Champaign, IL: Research Press.

Carlsson-Paige, N. (2001). Nurturing meaningful connections with young children. In L. Lantieri (Ed.), *Schools with spirit: Nurturing the inner lives of children and teachers* (pp. 21–38). Boston: Beacon Press.

Charles, C.M. (2007). *Building classroom discipline.* (9th ed.). New York: Longman.

Cushman, K. (2003). *Fires in the bathroom: Advice for teachers from high school students.* New York: The New Press.

Dewey, J. (1938). *Experience and education.* New York: Touchstone.

Dewey, J. (1944). *Democracy and education.* New York: Touchstone.

Dreikurs, R. (1968). *Psychology in the classroom* (2nd ed.). New York: Harper & Row.

Dreikurs, R., Cassel, P., & Ferguson, E. (2004). *Discipline without tears: How to reduce conflict and establish cooperation in the classroom.* Hoboken, NJ: Wiley.

Fagen, S. (1996). Fifteen teacher intervention skills for managing classroom behavior problems. In N. Long & W.C. Morse (Eds.), *Conflict in the classroom* (pp. 273–292). Austin, TX: PRO-ED.

Gladwell, M. (2000). *The tipping point: How little things can make a big difference.* New York: Little, Brown.

Glasser, W. (1998a). *Choice theory: A new psychology of personal freedom.* New York: HarperCollins.

Glasser, W. (1998b). *Choice theory in the classroom.* New York: HarperCollins.

Glasser, W. (1998c). *The quality school: Managing students without coercion.* New York: HarperCollins.

Glasser, W. (1998d). *The quality school teacher: A companion volume to the quality school.* New York: HarperCollins.

Goleman, D. (1995). *Emotional intelligence: Why it can matter more than IQ.* New York: Bantam Books.

Hartman, T. (1999). *The color code: A new way to see yourself, your relationships and life.* New Jersey: Scribner.

Hobbs, N. (1994). *The troubled and troubling child.* Cleveland, OH: American Re-Ed Association.

Jersild, A.T. (1955). *When teachers face themselves.* New York: Teachers College Press.

Keirsey, D., & Bates, M. (1984). *Please understand me: Character and temperament types* (3rd ed.). New York: Prometheus Nemesis Book Company.

King, M.L. Jr. (1959). *Stride toward freedom: The Montgomery story.* New York: Harper & Row.

Kohn, A. (1996). *Beyond discipline. From compliance to community.* Alexandria, VA: Association for Supervision and Curriculum Development.

Kounin, J. (1977). *Discipline and group management in classrooms* (Rev. ed.). New York: Holt, Rinehart & Winston.

Kushner, L. (2000). *Honey from the rock—Special anniversary edition.* Woodstock, VT: Jewish Lights Publishing.

Lantieri, L., & Patti, J. (1998). *Waging peace in our schools*. Boston: Beacon Press.

Larson, S., & Brendtro, L.K. (2000). *Reclaiming our prodigal sons and daughters: A practical approach for connecting with youth in conflict.* Bloomington, IN: National Educational Service.

Lickona, T. (2001). What is good character? And how can we develop it in our children? *Reclaiming Children and Youth, 9*(4), 239–251.

Lickona, T. (2004). *Character matters: How to help our children develop good judgment, integrity, and other essential virtues.* New York: Touchstone.

Long, N.J. (1997). The therapeutic power of kindness. *Reclaiming Children and Youth, 5*(4), 242–247.

Long, N.J. (2000). Personal struggles in reclaiming troubled students. *Reclaiming Children and Youth, 9*(2), 95–98.

Long, N.J. (2007). The conflict cycle paradigm: How troubled students get teachers out of control. In N.J. Long, W.C. Morse, F.A. Fescer, & R.G. Newman (Eds.), *Conflict in the classroom* (6th ed., pp. 325–350). Austin, TX: PRO-ED.

Long, N.J., Fecser, F.A., & Brendtro, L.K. (1998). Life space crisis intervention: New skills for reclaiming students showing patterns of self-defeating behavior. *Healing Magazine, 3*(2), 2–27.

Long, N., & Morse, W. (Eds.). (1996). *Conflict in the classroom: The education of at-risk and troubled students* (5th ed.). Austin, TX: PRO-ED.

Long, N.J., Morse, W.C., Fescer, F.A., & Newman, R.G. (Eds.). (2007). *Conflict in the classroom: Positive staff support for troubled students* (6th ed.). Austin, TX: PRO-ED.

Long, N.J., & Newman, R.G. (1996). The four choices of managing surface behavior of students. In N. Long & W.C. Morse (Eds.), *Conflict in the classroom* (pp. 266–273). Austin, TX: PRO-ED.

Long, N.J., Wood, M., & Fecser, F. (2001). *Life space crisis intervention: Talking with students in conflict* (2nd ed.). Austin, TX: PRO-ED.

Mand, C.L. (1983). Re-education through recreation. In L.K. Brendtro & A.E. Ness (Eds.), *Re-educating troubled youth: Environments for teaching and treatment.* Hawthorne, NY: Aldine de Gruyter.

Mendler, A., & Curwin, R. (1999). *Discipline with dignity for challenging youth.* Bloomington, IN: National Educational Service.

Monroe, L. (1995). Effective strategies for working with at-risk youth. In Boys Town Press (Eds.), *The on-going journey: Awakening spiritual life in at-risk youth* (pp. 155–169). Boys Town, Nebraska: Boys Town Press.

Myers, I.B. (1995). *Gifts differing: Understanding personality type.* New York: Davies-Black Publishing.

Nelsen, J., Lott, L., & Glenn, H.S. (2000). *Positive discipline in the classroom: Developing mutual respect, cooperation, and responsibility in your classroom* (3rd ed.). Rocklin, CA: Prima Publishing.

Nelson, J.R., Roberts, M.L., Mathur, S.R., & Rutherford, R.B. Jr. (1999). Has public policy exceeded our knowledge base? A review of the functional behavioral assessment literature. *Behavioral Disorders, 24,* 169–179.

Nicholas, M.P. (1995). *The lost art of listening: How learning to listen can improve relationships.* New York: Guilford.

Palmer, P. J. (1998). *The courage to teach.* San Francisco: Jossey-Bass.

Pascal, E. (1992). *Jung to live by: A guide to the practical application of Jungian principles for everyday life.* New York: Warner Books.

Phillips, D.T. (1999). *Martin Luther King, Jr. on Leadership: Inspirational Wisdom for Challenging Times.* New York: Warner.

Ravitch, D. (1985). *The schools we deserve: Reflections on the educational crises of our time.* New York: Basic Books.

Redl, F. (1959a). The concept of a therapeutic milieu. *American Journal of Orthopsychiatry, 29,* 721–734.

Redl, F. (1959b). The concept of life space interviewing. *American Journal of Orthopsychiatry, 29,* 1–18.

Redl, F. (1972). *When we deal with children.* New York: Free Press.

Redl, F., & Wattenberg, W. (1959). *Mental hygiene in teaching* (Rev. ed.). New York: Harcourt, Brace & World.

Redl, F., & Wineman, D. (1951). *Children who hate.* Glencoe, IL: Free Press.

Redl, F., & Wineman, D. (1952). *Controls from within.* Glencoe, IL: Free Press.

Seita, J.R., & Brendtro, L.K. (2002) *Kids who outwit adults.* Longmont, CO: Sopris West.

Shore, B. (1999). *The cathedral within: Transforming your life by giving something back.* New York: Random House.

Skinner, B.F. (1954). The science of learning and the art of teaching. *Harvard Educational Review, 24,* 86–97.

Skinner, B.F. (1973). The free and happy student. *Phi Delta Kappan, 55,* 13–16.

Starr Commonwealth. (2001). *Building safe and reclaiming schools.* Albion, MI: Author.

Szalavitz, M. (2006, January 29). The trouble with tough love. *The Washington Post,* pp. B1–B3.

Trulson, C., Triplett, R., & Snell, C. (2001). Social control in a school setting: Evaluating a school-based boot camp. *Crime and Delinquency, 47*(4), 573–609.

Vanzant, I. (2000). *Healthy mind, healthy body: A curriculum from the Inner Visions Institute for Spiritual Development.* Silver Spring, MD: Inner Visions Worldwide.

Ziedenberg, J., & Schiraldi, V. (2002). *Cellblocks or classrooms: The funding of higher education and corrections and its impact on African American men.* Washington, DC: Justice Policy Institute.

About the Author

EDNA OLIVE is a teacher, writer, consultant, facilitator, and coach dedicated to enhancing the lives of children and those who care for them. She is the founder and executive director of ROCKET, Inc., an educational consulting firm in Silver Spring, Maryland. Having planned to be an educator since the age of seven, her 25-year journey has led her to national and international forums, where she has served children, families, professionals, and organizations also dedicated to serving children and youth. She has spoken to and trained thousands of professionals throughout the United States and abroad. She holds graduate degrees from The George Washington University, including educational specialist and doctor of education. She sits on the board of directors of several organizations, including Reclaiming Youth International, Inc. She is a trainer in Positive Behavior Facilitation (PBF), a master trainer in Life Space Crisis Intervention (LSCI), and a trainer in Response Ability Pathways (RAP). She believes that serving today's children and youth must be a calling and that such service is part of a movement of which she is privileged to be a part.

ROCKET (Reaching Our Children with Knowledge, Expertise, and Teaching), Inc., provides services to organizations and all who support and care for children. ROCKET, Inc., believes that most children can (a) be reclaimed, (b) experience academic excellence, and (c) live successfully if those who support them are properly trained to do so. ROCKET, Inc., offers certificate programs in specialized training including Positive Behavior Facilitation (PBF). For more information, contact ROCKET, Inc. (rocketkids@comcast.net or www.rocketinc.net).